Archaeological Sites

Of Great Britain

RICKY DRINN

This book contains an A-Z OF Roman Villa's covering 32 counties along with an A-Z of Deserted Medieval villages covering 17 counties.

There is a section at the beginning of the book which covers the Yorkshire and Humber regions along with Lincolnshire and incorporates The Bronze age, The Iron age, The Roman period and the Late Medieval period.

All counties in the book are in alphabetical order and have been carefully researched from various sources and have been compiled into one great book.

The book is not intended for research purposes but has been put together for the benefit of the detectorist who can take it with them whenever and wherever they go metal detecting.

As a keen detectorist myself for 26 years I got frustrated at having to constantly write or print grid references down only to see them scattered all over the car floor or to have to risk taking a laptop or messing about with a mobile phone,

With this book you can look at all the sites and references in one place and have peace of mind that there are more than enough sites to try for permission on.

Please note that some of these sites will be scheduled but a large majority of them wont be so please remember it is up to the individual detectorist to find this information out prior to going on that land.

THE CODE OF CONDUCT FOR NATIONAL METAL DETECTING RELATING TO RESPONSIBLE PEOPLE

Do not trespass. Ask permission before venturing on to any private land.

Respect the country code. Do not leave gates open when crossing fields. Do not damage crops or frighten animals.

Do not leave a mess. it is perfectly simple to extract a coin or other small object buried a few inches under the ground without digging a large hole. Use a sharpened trowel or knife to cut a neat flap. Do not remove the plug of earth entirely from the ground. remove the object. replace the soil and grass carefully and even you would have difficulty finding the same spot again.

Help to keep Britain tidy....and help yourself. bottle tops, silver paper and cans are the last things you should throw away. you might well be digging them up the following year. Do yourself and the community a favour by taking the rusty iron and junk you find to the nearest litter bin.

If you discover any live ammunition or any lethal objects such as an unexploded bomb or mine. Do not touch it. Mark the spot carefully and report the find to the local police and landowners

Familiarize yourself with the law relating to archaeological sites. Remember it is illegal to use a metal detector on an ancient monument unless you are granted permission. Report all finds.

You are an ambassador to the hobby so be responsible.

Contents

East Yorkshire & Humber Regions

Deserted Medieval Villages

Roman Villas

Iron Age Sites

Barrows

Ring Ditches

Enclosures

Moated Sites

Pottery & Finds

North & Central Lincolnshire

Deserted Medieval Villages

Roman Villas

Iron Age Sites

Barrows

Ring Ditches

Enclosures

Moated Sites

Pottery & Finds

Roman Villas By County

Bedfordshire

Buckinghamshire

Cambridgeshire

Cheshire

Cornwall

Derbyshire

Devonshire

Dorset

Essex

Gloucestershire

Gtr London

Hampshire

Herefordshire

Hertfordshire

Isle Of Wight

Kent

Leicestershire

Lincolnshire

Norfolk

Northamptonshire

Nottinghamshire

Oxfordshire

Rutland

Shropshire

Somerset

Staffordshire

Suffolk

Surrey

Sussex

Warwickshire

Wiltshire

Worcestershire

Yorkshire

Wales

Deserted Medieval Villages By County

Berkshire

Buckinghamshire

Dorset

Gloucestershire

Herefordshire

Hertfordshire

Kent

Leicestershire

Lincolnshire

Norfolk

Oxfordshire

Rutland

Nottinghamshire

Sussex

Shropshire

Warwickshire

Wiltshire

East Yorkshire And The Humber

Beswick	**Enclosures & Ditches**	**TA 009484**
Bishop Burton	**Settlement Complexes**	**SE 985385**
		SE 988391
		SE 979391
Barrows & Hut Circles		**SE 955397**
		SE 952489
		SE 956489
	St Mary Magdalen Hospital	**TA 001395**
Killingwold Graves Founded Pre 1169		
	Large Complex Cropmark area	**SE 982392**
Settlement Complex/Ditched/Enclosures		**SE 968398**

	Roman Pots/Mortar Floors/Walls	SE 935272
	Coins of Claudius & Trajan	SE 935273
Cherry Burton	Settlement Cropmarks	SE 967420
Dalton Holme	Enclosures & Trackways	SE 963463
Eske	Deserted medieval Village	TA 056432
Etton	Settlement Cropmarks & Burials	SE 938432
Gardham	Deserted Medieval Village	SE 944414
Haltemprice	Deserted Medieval Village	TA 043310
Leconfield	Castle & Moated Site	TA 012431
Lockington	Motte & Bailey	TA 025411
Low Baswick	Settlement/ Cropmarks	TA 085467
North ferriby	Settlement/Foreshore	SE 982850

Ravensthorpe	Deserted Medieval Village	TA 006426
Riplingham	Deserted Medieval village	SE 960320
Rowley	Settlement Cropmarks	SE 958312
Scorborough	Settlement Cropmarks	TA 013450
Skidby	Settlement Cropmarks	SE 986315
South Cave	Tracks/Enclosures	SE 897298
		SE 897304
Welton Wold	Settlement Cropmarks	SE 983273
	Settlement/Cropmarks	SE 973282
	Settlement Cropmarks	SE 940340
Walkington	Settlement/Cropmarks	SE 984374
	Settlement & Burials	SE 997383
		SE 998378

Wawne	Settlement/Cropmarks	TA 099409
	Meaux Abbey Complexes	TA 092394
	Moated Site Complex	TA 099406
Woodmansey	Settlement/Burials	TA 043370
Cherry Burton	Ovoid Enclosures	TA 001421
	RB Wall Footings/1st Century Coins	SE 935276
	Trapezoid Enclosures	SE 939405
	Tumulus x 11	SE 941406
	Settlement site	SE 967420
	Sq Enclosure/Rounded Corners	SE 989432
	Ovoid Enclosure	TA 001421
	Former Old Manor House Site	SE 990421

Dalton holme	Settlement Complex/Enclosures	SE 932453
	Hut Circles & Settlement	SE 943464
	D Shaped Enclosure & Ditches	SE 961467
Etton	Complex Of Large Enclosures	SE 938432
	Enclosure Of Ovoid Shape	SE 946436
	DMV Of Arras	SE 934423
Haltemprice	Iron AgeTterret Found	TA 054321
	DMV Of Tranby	TA 025282
	Medieval Seal Found	TA 028259
	DMV Of Wolfreton	TA 036304
	Ancient Priory Site & DMV	TA 043310
	Roman Silver Brooch Found	TA 082344

Scorborough	Iron Age Square Barrow Cemetery	TA 019450
Leven	Large Extensive Enclosure Site	TA 085467
	Rectangular Enclosures	TA 118462
Lockington	RB Pottery Kilns	SE 998440
	Square Barrow Site	TA 029471
	DMV Of Lockington	SE 996469
	Extensive Medieval Site	SE 998465
	Iron Age RB Medieval Site	TA 001453
Lund	Iron Age Settlement & Burials	SE 932482
	DMV Of Enthorpe	SE 919464
Molescroft	Moated Site	TA 025411
N Newbald	Round Barrow site	SE 945392

	Rectangullar Enclosures	SE 946357
	Rectilinear Enclosures	SE 946399
	Large Enclosure Site	SE 948366
N Ferriby	RB Brooches Found	SE 976273
	La Tene Brooches Found	SE 986251
	Ovoid Enclosures	SE 980277
	Iron Age Pottery Found	SE 994253
	Iron Age Pottery Found	SE 997254
Rowley	Bronze Age Gold Bracelet	SE 956358
	Ovoid Enclosures	TA 003344
	DMV Of High Hunsley	SE 952351
	DMV Of Risby	TA 007349

Skidby	D Shaped Enclosure	SE 982320
	Extensive Enclosure Site	SE 986315
	Roman Tessarae Found	TA 021344
S. Cave	Large Enclosure Site	SE 897298
	Large Enclosure Site	SE 897304
	Ovoid Enclosures	SE 906310
	RB Settlement	SE 908293
	Large D Shaped enclosure	SE 934309
	Rectangular enclosure	SE 940340
	DMV of kettlethorpe	SE 916334
	DMV of Drewton	SE 925334
	DMV Of Weedley	SE 953331

Swanland	Round Barrow Sites	SE 990289
	Chapel Site Dating 1187	SE 993280
Ticton	Large RB Site	TA 059402
	DMV Of Storkhill	TA 050418
	DMV Of Eske	TA 056432
Walkington	Large Multi Period Site	SE 962357
	Large Earthwork Site	SE 971354
	Rectangular Enclosure	SE 970374
	Square Barrow Site	SE 984369
	Mixed Settlement Site	SE 998378
Wawne	Large Cropmark Site	TA 088407
	Extention Of Above Site	SE 091401

	DMV Of Wawne	TA 085368
	Meaux Abbey Site 1151AD	TA 092394
	DMV Of Meaux	TA 096403
Welton	Extensive Multi Settlement	SE 973282
	Multi Period Finds Made	SE 979249
	Ovoid Enclosure	SE 981290
	1st Cent Roman Dump Site	SE 982250
Blacktoft	Foreshore Site IA/RB [A]	SE 873254
	Knights Templar Site	SE 864249
Broomfleet	Foreshore Site [B]	SE 875258
Eastrington	DMV Of Thorpe Lidget	SE 765295
	Polygonal Enclosure	SE 782289

Ellerton	RB Pottery Found	SE 703401
	Gilbertine Priory 1209	SE 701399
Foggathorpe	Chapel Garth Moated Site	SE 762394
Gilberdyke	Rectangle & Polygonal Enclosures	SE 829300
	Roman Coin Finds	SE 836295
	DMV Of Owsthorpe	SE 810310
	DMV Of Greenoak	SE 815280
Holme upon Spalding Moor	Enclosures	SE 779364
	Enclosures	SE 781355
	RB kilns & Settlement	SE 795349
		SE 794348
	Hut Circles	SE 808332

	Square Enclosures x 3	SE 810355
	RB Kiln Site	SE 813337
	Large Ovoid Enclosure	SE 813393
	Group Of Rectangular Enclosures	SE 815343
	Settlements x 2	SE 818363
	Mixed Enclosures	SE 819329
	Trapezoidal Enclosure	SE 828374
	Ovoid Enclosure	SE 829375
	Rectangular Enclosure	SE 842384
	Large Settlement Site	SE 846354
Kilpin	Roman Lead Pig Found	SE770285
	DMV Of Belby	SE 771290

	DMV Of West Lynton	SE 793280
	DMV Of East Lynton	SE 800283
Laxton	DMV Of Cotness	SE 800240
	DMV Of Meth	SE 810248
North cave	IA & RB Settlement	SE 877321
	Settlement Cropmarks	SE 883333
Aldbrough	Polygonal Enclosure	TA 223376
	Rectangular Enclosure	TA 246393
	DMV Of Fosham	TA 209388
	DMV Of Etherdwick	TA 231373
	DMV Of Bewick	TA 233395
	DMV Of Ringborough	TA 273375

	DMV of Arram	TA 165493
	DMV Of High Skirlington	TA 180525
Bewholme	St Mary Magdalene Priory	TA 145501
	DMV Of Nunkeeling	TA 143502
	DMV Of Bonwick	TA 165525
Brandesburton	Rectangular Enclosure	TA 108473
	IA Pottery Found Here	TA 123475
	St Nichola's Chapel	TA 083493
	Balkhill Moated Site	TA 085504
Burstwick	Rectangular Enclosure	TA 217286
	DMV Of Nuthill	TA 215300
	DMV Of Lund Garth	TA 203316

	DMV Of Skeckling	TA 220280
	DMV Of Bond Burstwick	TA 220290
	DMV Of Totleys	TA 239274
Burton Constable	DMV Of Burton Constable	TA 190368
	DMV 0f West Newton	TA 203378
Easington	RB Settlement	TA 408187
	RB Pottery Found Here	TA 409186
East Garton	DMV Of Garton	TA 263355
	DMV Of Grimston	TA 277357
	Enclosure Site	TA 277362
Ellerby	DMV Of Dowthorpe	TA 154381
	DMV Of Old Ellerby	TA 168380

Elstronwick	**DMV Of Dyke**	**TA 213335**
	Rectangular Enclosure	**TA 222327**
	Polygonal Enclosure	**TA 247333**
Hatfield	**DMV Of Little Hatfield**	**TA 173432**
	DMV Of Goxhill	**TA 185450**
	Old St Helens church	**TA 187426**
	Moated Site	**TA 190429**
Hedon	**St Sepulchre's Hospital**	**TA 189292**
	St Jame's Church	**TA 188283**
	St Nichola's Church	**TA 192285**
Hornsea	**Gold Staters Found Here**	**TA 207475**
	DMV Of Southorpe	**TA 196464**

	DMV Of Hornsey Beck	TA 212484
Humbleton	Rectangular Enclosure	TA 213346
	DMV Of Flinton	TA 220361
	DMV Of Humbleton	TA 227344
Keyingham	RB Skeletons & Pots	TA 236253
	Roman Coins Found Here	TA 239249
	Roman Pottery Found	TA 237261
	Trapezoid Enclosure	TA 222235
	Moated Site	TA 230243
Mappleton	Gold Staters Found Here	TA 219413
	DMV Of Mappleton	TA 223443
	DMV Of Great Cowden	TA 237423

	DMV Of Little Cowden	TA 238426
Preston	Square Enclosure	TA 194324
	DMV Of Preston	TA 174302
	Moated Site	TA 181305
Rimswell	Moated Site	TA 323285
	DMV Of Newsham	TA 305268
Rise	DMV Of Rise	TA 156423
Riston	DMV Of Long Riston	TA 124426
Roos	DMV Of Monkwith	TA 300328
	Moated Site	TA 305322
Seaton	DMV Of Catfoss	TA 143467
Sigglesthorne	DMV Of Sigglesthorne	TA 157458

Skirlaugh	DMV Of Rowton	TA 138402
Sproatley	DMV Of Sproatley	TA 196333
Swine	Rectilinear Enclosure	TA 123368
	IA Sq Barrow Cemetery	TA 128392
	Roman Coin Hoard Found	TA 135354
	DMV Of West Beningholme	TA 118388
	DMV Of East Beningholme	TA 127387
	St Marys Ppriory	TA 132358
	DMV Of Swine	TA 136359
Thorngumbald	DMV Of Camerton	TA 216262
	Large Settlement	TA 221268
	Moated Site	TA 218260

Welwick	DMV Of Welwick	TA 333216
	DMV Of Penisthorpe	TA 345210
Withernwick	DMV Of Withernwick	TA 198408

NORTH WOLDS AREA

Allerthorpe	Roman Pottery Found	TA 748477
	Rectilinear Enclosures	SE 767468
		SE 771461
	Rectangular Enclosure	SE 778478
	Building & Enclosure	SE 788462
	Polygonal Enclosure	SE 796472
	DMV Of Waplington	SE775465
Bainton	Hut Site	SE 943536

	Rectangular Enclosures	SE 951523
		SE 952524
	RB Pottery Found Here	SE 952509
	DMV Of Bainton	SE 960523
	DMV Of Neswick	SE 974528
Barmston	Settlement Site	TA 155633
	Settlement Site	TA 169606
	DMV Of Wincton	TA 153603
	DMV Of Barmston	TA 156589
	DMV Of Auburn	TA169627
	DMV Of Hartburn	TA 170613
Beeford	Skeletons Found	TA 108550

	Ring Ditches	TA 120554
	Old Garths Settlement	TA 135645
	Moated Site	TA 139512
Bempton	Enclosure Complexes	TA 167722
		TA 168722
		TA 173716
	Pits & Hut Circles	TA 167737
	Round Barrows	TA 171746
	Rectangular Enclosure	TA 176726
	Ring Ditches [High Barn]	TA 190708
	Round Barrow Site	TA 192717
	Large Rect Enclosure	TA 197706

	Large Square Barrow	TA 202730
	DMV Of Buckton	TA 183726
	DMV Of Newsham	TA 190719
	DMV Of Marton	TA 202700
Bishop Wilton	Enclosures	TA 744537
	Tumulus	SE 780565
	Triangular Enclosures	SE 795445
	Tumulus	SE 808565
	Tumulus	SE 808567
	Ring Ditches	SE 812550
	Anglian Burials	SE 812563
	Barrow Site	SE 814456

	Ring Ditches	SE 824564
	Moated Site	SE 780541
	Archbishops Palace	SE 800553
Boynton	Hut Circles	SE 121706

Multi Complex Settlement Sites & Enclosures

	TA 122674
	TA 123675
	TA 122672
	TA 128674
	TA 123674
	TA 124675
Settlement Enclosures	TA 122685

Rectilinear Enclosure	TA 122703
Tesselated Pavement	TA 122706
Carnaby Tenple Site	TA 136670
	TA 136671
Ring Ditches	TA 124694
	TA 123692
RB & Anglian Settlement	TA 128676
	TA 128677
	TA 129676
Roman Coins Of Lucilla	TA 138703
Large Enclosure	TA 139685
Rectilinear Enclosures	TA 143684

		TA 144690
	Rectangular Enclosure	TA 157701
	DMV Of Easton	TA 153680
Bridlington	Coins Of Hadrian & Carausius	TA 182683
	RB Pottery & Querns Found	TA 202689
	DMV Of Hilderthorpe	TA 174656
	Saxon Silver Halfpenny	TA 182685
	DMV Of Sewerby	TA 202691
	DMV Of Marton	TA 203699
Bugthorpe	Rectilinear Enclosure	SE 762569
	Trapezoid Enclosure	SE 769573
	Ovoid Enclosures	SE 772572

		SE 772570
	Enclosures & Tracks	SE 778582
Burton Agnes	IA Settlement	TA 089650
	Settlement Complex	TA 091653
	Rectangular Enclosures	TA 095645
	Ring Ditches	TA 095653
	IA Settlement Complex	TA 111596
	Large Square Enclosure	TA 113656
	IA & RB Settlement Site	TA 131603
	Polygonal Enclosure	TA 105656
	Large Square Enclosure	TA 113656
	Large IA Sq Barrow Cemetery	TA 130619

	DMV Of Old Garths	TA 120595
Burton Fleming	Complex Settlement Sites	TA 089712
		TA 069703
		TA 097715
		TA 076713
		TA 073686
		TA 078708
	Square Barrows & Enclosures	TA 092703
	D Shaped Enclosure & Ovoid Enclosure	TA 092726
	Square Barrow Cemetery	TA 094720
	Hut Circle Site	TA 108718
Carnaby	Large Square Barrow Cemetery	TA 130622
	Rectilinear Enclosures	TA 133631
	Large Linear Settlement Site	TA 106715
	Settlement Enclosures	TA 165636

	DMV Of Haisthorpe	TA 129643
	DMV Of Carnaby	TA 147653
	DMV Of Wilsthorpe	TA 169640
Catton	Settlement Enclosure With Huts	SE 719533
	Butt Hills Moated Site	SE 704539
	Ring Ditches x 10	SE 716531
	Grade 2 Henge Monument	SE 721534
	Small Group Of Enclosures	SE 716508
Cottam	Willy Howe Tumulus	SE 955659
	Large Ovoid Enclosure	SE 957654
	Large IA Square Barrow Cemetery	TA 130622
	Rectangular Enclosures	SE 962647

Kemp Howe Round Barrow	**SE 962663**
10.000 4th Cent Roman Coins Found	**SE 968653**
Rectilinear Enclosures	**SE 969647**
Rectilinear Enclosures	**SE 977688**
Rectilinear Enclosures	**SE 984657**
IA Settlement With Group Of Square Barrows **Early LA Tene Bracelets & Brooches**	**SE 984667**
Rectilinear Enclosures	**SE 988653**
	SE 993657
	TA 001640
DMV Of Cowlam	**TA 966656**
DMV Of Cottam	**TA 993647**

Driffield	Large Enclosure	TA 040575
	Rectangular Enclosure	TA 030571
	Enclosures & Hut Circles	TA 029597
	Cheesecake Hill Tumulus	TA 043578
	Bronze Age & Anglian Remains	TA 020575
		TA 023576
	Moot Hill Round Barrow	TA 024583
	Chapel Nook Burial Grounds	TA 027567
	Large Rectilinear Enclosure	TA 030571
Everingham	Group Of Rectilinear Enclosures	SE 804400
	Subdivided Enclosure	SE 827425
	Large Rectangular Enclosure	SE 832415

	Rectangular Enclosure	SE 834424
	Ring Ditches	SE 834418
	Very Large Enclosures x 2	SE 828410
Fangfoss	Enclosures	SE 748536
	Large polygonal	SE 754517
	Enclosures & Hut Circles	SE 758511
	Moated Site Known As Hall Garth	SE 772521
Fimber	Groups Of Tumulus	SE 880637
		SE 882640
		SE 884641
		SE 885641
		SE 888641

		SE 891610
	Square Barrows & Settlement	SE 892642
	Tumulus	SE 892643
	Bronze age Barrow Multiple Occupation	SE 894606
	Square Barrows	SE 894611
		SE 893611
	Tumulus	SE 896645
	DMV Of Fimber	SE 893605
		SE 895604
	DMV Of Towthorpe	SE 898629
Flamborough	Ring Ditch	TA 218701
	Tumulus	TA 219720

	Large Rectilinear Enclosure	TA 223696
	RB Settlement Site	TA 225693
	Large Ring Ditches	TA 235698
	Tumulus	TA 246699
Foston	Group Of Rectilinear Enclosures	TA 075550
	Rectangular Enclosure	TA 104552
	DMV Of Brigham	TA 077536
	Moated Site	TA 078526
Garton	Garton Slack Extensive IA	SE 953600
	& Roman Burial Site Incorporating	
	Settlements & Agricultural Sites	SE 949599
	With Hut Circles Ring Ditches	
	Round & Square Barrows & Cart	SE 949602
	Burials	
	Settlement Enclosures	SE 956595

Tumulus	SE 957583
	SE 957597
	SE 959588
	SE 960584
	SE 960585
	SE 961583
	SE 961584
	SE 962580
	SE 962588
	SE 963580
	SE 963582
Rectilinear Enclosure	SE 981603

	Ring Ditch	SE 983612
	Large Rectangular Enclosure	SE 984610
	Ring Ditch	SE 987605
	Rectangular Enclosure	SE 995596
	DMV Of Garton	SE 976597
	Ancient Enclosure	TA 001597
Goodmanham	Round Barrow Site	SE 882434
	Enclosure With Circle	SE 882435
	Rectangular Enclosure	SE 883383
	Roman Coins & Pottery	SE 884426
	Large Settlement Complex	SE 900444
	Large Barrow Site	SE 912457

Grindale	**Large Ring Ditch**	**TA 107713**
	Rectangular Enclosure	**TA 109711**
	Large Group Of Enclosures	**TA 110720**
	Complex Settlement Area	**TA 124713**
	Ring Ditch	**TA 126720**
	Roman Villa	**TA 135713**
	Group Of Rectilinear Enclosures	**TA 135725**
	Group Of Rectilinear Settlements	**TA 140727**
	Square Barrow Cemetery	**TA 143711**
	Large Square Barrow Cemetery	**TA 148720**
	Ring Ditch	**TA 157715**
	DMV Of Argam	**TA 113713**

	DMV Of Grindale	TA 132709
Harpham	Roman Villa	TA 090636
	Rectangular & Polygonal Enclosures	TA 071602
	Large Area Of Extensive Settlements	TA 077588
		TA 082588
		TA 085589
		TA 088592
	Ring Ditch	TA 088588
Huggate	Large Group Of Barrows	SE 840569
		SE 841570
		SE 843571
		SE 848571

Large Group Of Round Barrows	**SE 858538**
	SE 858539
	SE 860539
Group Of Ring Ditches	**SE 858571**
RB Rectangular Enclosure	**SE 883567**
Settlement Site	**SE 883575**
Ring Ditches x2	**SE 892549**
Large Group Of 22 Round Barrows	
Jarvis Lands	**SE 900549**
	SE 901550
	SE 900548
Squared Enclosure	**SE 906568**
RB Hut	**SE 909579**

	Group Of Barrows	SE 914551
		SE 912552
	Rectilinear Settlement	SE 917574
	Rectilinear Settlement	SE 918579
	Tumulus	SE 922557
	Large Square Barrow Cemetery	SE 925557
	DMV Of Huggate	SE 881556
Hutton Cranswick	Ring Ditch	TA 012554
	Round Barrow	TA 020560
	DMV Of Sunderlandwick	TA 011551
	DMV Of Skibedon	TA 016526
	Moated Site	TA 032521

	Moated Site	TA 024516
	DMV Of Rotsea	TA 062518
	Lake Dwelling Site	TA 107601
	Group Of Enclosures	TA 114588
	Medieval Pottery Kiln Site	TA 097601
	DMV Of Great Kelk	TA 100590
Kilham	Ring Ditch	TA 004642
	Enclosure	TA 004649
	Round Barrow	TA 006636
	Large Complex Settlement Site	TA 013637
	Large Rectlinear Enclosure	TA 011647
	Square Barrow Group	TA 017641

Rectilinear Enclosures	TA 024641
	TA 024646
Ring Ditch	TA 029688
Enclosure	TA 034661
Large Polygonal Enclosure	TA 037694
Ring Ditch	TA 048649
Rectangular Enclosure	TA 048689
Large Extensive Settlement Site	TA 050660
Long Barrow	TA 056673
Square Barrow Cemetery	TA 068661
Square Barrows	TA 076670
Hut Circle Site	TA 078661

	Large Extensive Settlement Site	TA 085655
	DMV Of Swaythorpe	TA 038690
	DMV Of Killham	TA 054643
	Medieval Burial Site	TA 063643
Kirby Underdale	Round Barrow	TA 802590
	RB Settlement	SE 814569
	Barrow Group	SE 815569
	Tumulus	SE 832570
	Tumulus	SE 832578
	Tumulus	SE 832580
	Tumulus	SE 842573
	Tumulus	SE 970577

DMV Of Garroby	**SE 795574**
DMV Of Uncleby	**SE 811591**
DMV Of Painsthorpe	**SE 813583**
Bronze Age Settlement	**SE 972576**
Rectilinear Settlement	**SE 973558**
Long Barrow	**SE 978577**
Ring Ditch	**SE 980575**
Long Barrow	**SE 979576**
Subrectangular Enclosure	**SE 981577**
Late Roman Kilns	**SE 986559**
IA Square Barrow Cemetery	**TA 004565**
DMV Of Kirkburn	**TA 977550**

	DMV Of Low Battleburn	TA 986554
	DMV Of Southburn	TA 989542
	DMV Of Eastburn	TA 991555
	DMV Of Kelleythorpe	TA 012565
Langtoft	Rectilinear Enclosure	SE 991660
	Enclosure Within Enclosure	SE 996656
	RB Corn Drying Kiln	SE 999660
	Rectilinear Complex	SE 000658
	Square Barrows	SE 013653
	Settlement Complex	SE 016656
	Rectilinear Enclosures	SE 018675
	Settlement Enclosures	SE 023682

	Rectilinear Enclosures	SE 023682
	Moated Site	SE 852460
	RB Buildings	SE 865444
	Rectangular Enclosure	SE 866468
	DMV Of Towthorpe	SE 867438
	DMV Of Eastthorpe	SE 880454
Market Weighton	Rectilinear Enclosure	SE 859414
	Roman Coins	SE 861423
	Enclosures	SE 865410
	Complex Settlement	SE 866395
	Square Enclosure	SE 868404
	Roman Coins	SE 868416

RB Pottery	SE 877438
Roman Coins	SE 872409
Silver Denarius Of Trajan	SE 876426
Roman Brooch	SE 879419
Roman Coins & Pottery	SE 880402
Rectangular Enclosure	SE 880435
Settlement Site	SE 892422
Barrows	SE 893415
Group Of Ring Ditches	SE 896421
Long Barrow Group	SE 907410
Large Barrow Group	SE 908413
Rectangular Enclosure	SE 913422

	Large IA Square Barrow Cemetery	SE 929414
	DMV Of Arras	SE 923417
Middleton	Ring Ditch	SE 892481
	Settlement	SE 895475
	Ring Ditch	SE 901475
	Rectilinear Enclosures	SE 915482
	Rectangular Enclosure	SE 919490
	Large IA Square Barrow Cemetery	SE 922494
	Settlement Complex	SE 929502
	Large Settlement Site	SE 934488
	IA & Roman Burial Site	SE 944495
	DMV Of Kippling cotes	SE 898476

Millington	Ring Ditch	SE 807532
	IA Burials & Hill Fort	SE 816535
	Ring Ditch	SE 817545
	Large Rectangular Enclosure	SE 820535
	Roman Cemetery	SE 823517
	Roman Settlement & Coins	SE 839529
	Tunulus	SE 840560
	Ring Ditch	SE 840567
	Hut Site	SE 842542
	Tumulus	SE 859563
	DMV Of Grimthorpe	SE 812529
	DMV Of Ousethorpe	SE 820515

	Moated Site	SE 813512
	DMV Of Little Givendale	SE 823531
	Rectangular Enclosures	SE 843541
Nafferton	Rectilinear Settlement	TA 008628
	Square Barrows	TA 009623
	Rectilinear Enclosures	TA 012615
	Settlement Enclosure Complex	TA 012626
	Settlement Complex	TA 015615
	IA Settlement	TA 018602
	Extensive Square Barrow Cemetery	TA 018633
	Rectangular Enclosure	TA 028635
	Rectilinear Enclosure	TA 026624

	Large Settlement Site	TA 029629
	Ring Ditch	TA 030610
	Bronze Sword Found	TA 063579
	Rectangular Enclosure	TA 076567
	DMV Of Pockthorpe	TA 040634
North Dalton	Tumulus	SE 903517
	Enclosure	SE 903544
	Enclosures	SE 907528
	Rectilinear Enclosure	SE 912543
	Enclosure	SE 923520
	Square Barrows	SE 941542
	Rectangular Enclosure	SE 935539

	Square Barrows	SE 927537
	Rectangular Enclosure	SE 926537
	Group Of Enclosures	SE 932514
	Tumulus	SE 936524
	Rectilinear Enclosures	SE 941534
	Large Settlement Complex	SE 943513
	DMV Of North Dalton	SE 933523
Nunburnholme	Round Barrows	SE 817505
	Roman Pottery	SE 842503
	Enclosure	SE 860478
	Square Barrows	SE 862471
	Roman Coin Hoard	SE 867491

	Rectilinear Enclosures	SE 868473
	Square Barrows	SE 868480
	Square Barrow Cemetery	SE 873482
	Square Barrows	SE 874483
	DMV Of Kilnwick Percy	SE 827497
	Medieval Nunnery	SE 853484
Pocklington	Roman Coins	SE 796497
	Rectangular Enclosure	SE 801461
	Rectangular Enclosure	SE 803460
	Hut Site	SE 803469
	Square Barrow	SE 808482
	Rectilinear Enclosures	SE 811473

	Roman Pottery	SE 818488
	Roman Coins	SE 818491
Rudston	Settlement Complex	TA 057684
	Settlement Complex	TA 060691
	Rectilinear Enclosure	TA 066687
	Long Barrows	TA 076678
	Ring Ditch	TA 077669
	Extensive Settlement Site	TA 079675
	Extensive Settlement Site	TA 081691
	Rectangular Enclosure	TA 083685
	Settlement Site	TA 086694
	Roman Villa	TA 089667

Ring Ditch	TA 089687
Settlement Enclosures	TA 090657
Square Barrows	TA 093701
Rectilinear Settlement	TA 094685
Large IA Square Barrow Cemetery	TA 094695
Enclosure	TA 096696
Square Barrows	TA 098685
Settlement Complex	TA 098695
Square Barrows	TA 099658
Complex Settlement	TA 099671
Settlement Site	TA 097680
Ring Ditch Group	TA 105661

	Hill Fort	TA 115684
	Settlement Enclosures	TA 115682
	Rectangular Enclosure	TA 118686
	Group Of Ring Ditches	TA 118686
	DMV Of Rudston	TA 097675
	Medieval Pottery	TA 098678
	DMV Of Thorpe	TA 110678
	DMV Of Low Caythorpe	TA 118678
Sancton	Roman Coins	SE 899400
	Tumulus	SE 908409
	Ring Ditch	SE 910391
	Tumulus	SE 924401

	Tumulus	SE 930408
	Rectangular Enclosure	SE 932402
	DMV Of Houghton	SE 888387
	DMV Of Hessleskew	SE 926403
Skerne	Rectangular Enclosure	TA 046565
	Settlement Complex	TA 051563
	Rectilinear Enclosure	TA 060565
	Roman Coin Hoard	TA 067550
	DMV Of Skerne	TA 044551
	Rectangular Enclosures	TA 064568
Skipsea	Rectangular Enclosure	TA 140548
	Moated Site	TA 139545

	DMV Of Dringhoe	TA 157552
	Moated Site	TA 162551
	Moated Site	TA 170546
	DMV Of Cleeton	TA 190543
Skirpenbeck	Ring Ditches	SE 733577
	Tumulus	SE 737580
	Barrow	SE 739572
	Square Barrows	SE 745582
	Moated Site	SE 750573
Sledmere	Round Barrow	SE 917652
	Ring Ditch	SE 924604
	Rectangular Enclosure	SE 925619

	Tumulus	SE 925621
	Tumulus	SE 927621
	Tumulus	SE 936619
	Tumulus	SE 944621
	Round Barrows	SE 947622
	Tumulus	SE 955624
	DMV Of Sledmere	SE 930648
	DMV Of Croom	SE 935658
South Cliffe	Rectilinear Enclosure	SE 846372
	Rectilinear Enclosure	SE 855364
	Extensive Settlement Complex	SE 866363
	Rectangular Enclosure	SE 868352

	Enclosures	SE 888358
Stamford Bridge	Roman Fort	SE 715555
	Rectangular Enclosure	SE 719556
	DMV Of Hundeburton	SE 725557
	Trapezoidal Enclosure	SE 877351
Thwing	Tumulus	SE 005691
	IA/Bronze Age Pottery	SE 013700
	Ring Ditches	SE 024715
	Square Barrows	SE 028707
	Bronze Age Defended Site	SE 031707
	Ring Ditches	SE 032718
	Rectangular Enclosure	SE 033713

	Square Barrow Cemetery	SE 036713
	Square Barrows	SE 039709
	Rectangular Enclosure	SE 042719
	Roman Pottery	SE 047701
	Ring Ditch	SE 048716
	Tumulus	SE 051721
	Rectilinear Enclosure	SE 057706
	Settlement Complex	SE 058696
	Large Barrow	SE 062724
	DMV Of Octon	SE 033700
	DMV Of Thwing	SE 048702
Tibthorpe	Settlement Enclosure	SE 930548

	Square Barrow Cemetery	SE 930567
	Settlement Enclosures	SE 943543
	Square Barrows	SE 950572
	Rectilinear Enclosures	SE 953556
	Bronze Age Pottery	SE 959579
	DMV Of Tibthorpe	SE 958553
Warter	Ring Ditch	SE 838514
	Ring Ditch	SE 841518
	Tumulus	SE 843520
	Square Barrows	SE 843510
	Tumulus	SE 843520
	Square Barrows	SE 848521

	Roman Coins	SE 873503
	Circular Enclosure	SE 873527
	Barrows	SE 899532
	Warter Priory	SE 870505
	DMV Of Rickman	SE 873505
Watton	Rectangular Enclosure	SE 974505
	Bronze Age Site	TA 036493
	Round Barrow	TA 056492
	DMV Of Bracken	TA 984502
	DMV Of Watton	TA 018501
	Watton Priory	TA 023499
Wetwang	Rectilinear Enclosures	SE 892584

	Rectangular Enclosure	SE 900584
	Group Of Ring Ditches	SE 904585
	Extensive Settlement Site	SE 904588
	Extensive Settlement Site	SE 919597
	Settlement Site	SE 932603
	Square Barrows	SE 943582
	Complex Settlement Site	SE 953582
	DMV Of Holm	SE 878582
	DMV Of Wetwang	SE 935592
Wilberfoss	Square Enclosure	SE 747514
	Complex Settlement	SE 758509
	Moated Site	SE 732511

	Benedictine Nunnery	SE 733510
Wold Newton	Enclosure	TA 028740
	Ring Ditches	TA 031750
	Barrows	TA 031758
	Ring Ditch	TA 033760
	Ring Ditches	TA 036742
	Tumulus	TA 048726
	Hut Circle	TA 052730
	Large Extensive Settlement	TA 059748
	Group Of Ring Ditches	TA 060744
	Duntze Dale Settlement	TA 041767
	DMV Of Fordon	TA 049752

Adlingfleet	**Moated Site**	**SE 842211**
Amcotts	**DMV Of Amcotts**	**SE 850166**
Belton	**Large RB Settlement Site**	**SE 734090**
	Medieval Pottery	**SE 778089**
	Medieval Pottery	**SE 798072**
	Medieval Pottery	**SE 809073**
	Medieval Pottery	**SE 811074**
	Moated Site	**SE 816073**
	Knights Templar Site	**SE 799089**
	Ring Ditch	**SE 813062**
Crowle	**Dmv Of Tetley**	**SE 776116**

	Roman Pottery	SE 778127
Eastoft	Roman Pottery	SE 799144
Epworth	Rectilinear Enclosure	SE 788044
	Rectangular Enclosure	SE 802047
Fockerby	Moated Site	SE 839194
Garthorpe	Roman coin	SE 849189
	DMV Of Waterton	SE 853180
Haldenby	DMV Of Haldenby	SE 827184
Haxey	Multiperiod Site	SE 770020
	Roman Pottery	SE 785021
	DMV Of High Burnham	SE 784021
Keadby	Roman Pottery Site	SE 827087

Ousefleet	Moated Site	SE 825229
Owston Ferry	Roman Coin Hoard	SE 79340108
	Roman Pottery	SE 80650110
	Moated Site	SE 805003
	Melwood Priory	SE 809019
	Monastic Building	SE 798982
	Medieval Chapel	SE 812998
Ashby Cum Fenby	Roman Pottery	TA 242013
	Moated Site	TA 253010
	DMV Of Fenby	TA 260993
Aylesby	Roman Pottery	TA 202070
	DMV Of Aylesby	TA 204074

	Medieval Pottery	TA 227082
	Enclosure	TA 196065
Barnoldby Le Beck	DMV Of Barnoldby	TA 235029
Beelsby	Long Barrow	TA 189010
	Round Barrow	TA 19950064
	DMV Of Beelsby	TA 208018
	Rectangular Enclosures	TA 215023
Bradley	DMV Of Bradley	TA 240065
Cleethorpes	Coritani Gold Stater	TA 30570770
	Roman Pottery	TA 30520947
	Roman Coins	TA 29580984
	Roman Coins	TA 30570930

	Roman Coins	TA 30730913
	Roman Coins	TA 30670925
	Roman Coins	TA 29990977
	DMV Of Thrunscoe	TA 312076
East Ravendale	DMV Of East Ravendale	TA 237991
Habrough	DMV Of Habrough	TA 145135
	Rectilinear Enclosure	TA 136144
	Enclosure	TA 152147
Hatcliffe	Roman Pottery	TA 230020
	DMV Of Gunnerby	TA 215990
	Rectangular Enclosure	TA 214005
Hawerby Cum Beesby	Round Barrow	TA 25349764

	Roman Pottery	TA 261958
	DMV Of Beesby	TA 266966
	DMV Of Hawerby	TA 262976
Healing	Moated Site	TA 213099
Humberston	Benedictine Abbey	TA 31050514
Immingham	Roman Coins	TA 176151
	DMV Of Immingham	TA 173149
	DMV Of Roxton	TA 168127
	Moated Site	TA 190134
Irby On Humber	Roman Pottery	TA 209036
	Roman Building	TA 209039
	Moated Site	TA 212043

	Rectangular Enclosure	TA 213042
Stallingborough	DMV Of Stallingborough	TA 195115
	Moated Site	TA 195118
	Medieval Pottery	TA 181118
	Rectangular Enclosure	TA 209124
	DMV Of Houflet	TA 238130
West Ravendale	DMV Of West Ravendale	TF 227997
	Ravendale Priory	TF 226996
Wold Newton	DMV Of Wold Newton	TF 243965
Alkborough	DMV Of Walcot	SE 879208
	Rectangular Enclosure	SE 896203
Appleby	Tumulus	SE 944127

	Bronze Age Weapon Hoard	SE 94891640
	Roman Pottery	SE 944147
	Roman Coins	SE 95231488
	DMV Of Santon	SE 940129
	Augustinian Priory	SE 965125
	Rectangular Buildings	SE 946162
	Rectangular Enclosure	SE 930127
Barnetby Le Wold	Circular Enclosures	TA 075105
Barrow Upon Humber	Barrows	TA 042181
	Bronze Axe	TA 087210
	RB Site	TA 952190
	Moated Site	TA 066225

	Long Barrows	TA 066225
Bottesford	Bronze Axe & Spearhead	TA 88110692
	RB Pottery & Artefacts	TA 90070726
	Knights Templar Site	TA 897070
	DMV Of Bottesford	TA 898070
Brigg	Roman Coins	TA 002084
Broughton	Barrow Cemetery	SE 966107
	Roman Brooches	SE 955086
	Roman Pottery	SE 942084
	Medieval Pottery	SE 96310868
	Moated Site	SE 987077
	Cistercian nunnery	SE 941102

	DMV Of Manby	SE 936088
	Ring Ditch	SE 979105
Burringham	Roman Coins	SE 83430931
Burton Upon Stather	RB Site	SE 88421733
	Roman Pottery	SE 88261735
	Roman Brooches	SE 878161
	Roman Seal Box	SE 871164
	Roman Coins	SE 87451735
	Roman Coins	SE 890170
	Roman Coins	SE 87101785
	Moated Site	SE 88451655
	DMV Of Darby	SE 876180

Cadney Cum Howsham	RB Site	TA 041048
	Roman Pottery	TA 04680426
	Newstead Priory	TA 000045
Croxton	DMV Of Croxton	TA 097122
	Enclosures	TA 099133
	Ring Ditch	TA 079122
East Halton	Roman Pottery	TA 128208
	Roman Pottery	TA 135195
	Roman Pottery	TA 138190
	Moated Site	TA 140201
	Moated Site	TA 142188
Elsham	Moated Site	TA 029114

	Rectangular Enclosure	TA 048112
	Enclosure	TA 018121
Hibaldstowe	IA & RB Settlement	SE 960030
	Roman Building Rubble	SE 963028
	Tesselated Pavement	SE 968033
	Roman Coins	SE 95050203
	DMV Of Gainsthorpe	SE 956011
	Rectangular Enclosure	SE 980018
	Ring Ditch	SE 977011
Holme	Hut Site	SE 910056
	Roman Coin	SE 90650697
	DMV Of Raventhorpe	SE 936079

	DMV Of Holme	SE 908068
	Rectangular Enclosure	SE 909053
	Enclosures	SE 903056
	Enclosures	SE 903062
	Large Enclosure	SE 917065
	Enclosure	SE 904069
	Complex Sites	SE 910073
		SE 910074
Horkstow	Mosaic Pavements	SE 98501914
	Edward 1 Penny	TA 001179
	DMV Of Horkstow	SE 986183
Kirmington	Multi Settlement	TA 09551120

	Roman Coins	TA 097111
	Large Roman Coin Hoard	TA 095115
	Roman Coins	TA 106114
	Complex Site	TA 092105
Kirton In Lindsey	Round Barrow	SK 927981
	Roman Villa	SE 939004
	Roman Coins	SK 932986
	Roman Pavement	SK 932987
	Moated Site	SK 932985
	Oval Enclosure	SK 95019859
	Oval Enclosure	SK 936974
Manton Warren	RB Hut Site	SE 939037

	RB Cremation Cemetery	SE 940034
	DMV Of Manton	SE 934026
	DMV Of Cleatham	SE 933010
	Enclosure	SE 926037
	Large Enclosure	SE 928042
	Rectangular Enclosure	SE 932041
	Rectilinear Enclosure	SE 926018
	Rectangular Enclosures	SE 925040
Melton Ross	Moated Site	TA 072105
	Rectangular Enclosure	TA 056115
	Rectangular Enclosure	TA 057116
	Enclosure	TA 057110

	Enclosure	TA 075105
Messingham	Looped Palstave Axe	SE 88050567
	Socketed Axe	SE 84740330
	Socketed Axes x 2	SE 89200280
	Looped Axe & Spearhead	SE 87090443
	Socketed Spearhead	SE 866057
	Roman Coins	SE 866057
	RB Settlement	SE 907038
	Roman Pottery	SE 907052
	Roman Rubble & Pottery	SE 901062
	Roman Domestic Dump	SE 89100486
	Moated Site	SE 891045

	Rectangular Enclosure	SE 894057
	Enclosures	SE 902056
	Roman Buildings	SE 901060
North Killingholme	DMV Of Holtham	TA 148168
	Roman Pottery	TA 155178
		TA 151180
		TA 164175
		TA 166180
	Roman Quern Stone	TA 138163
	DMV Of N.Killingholme	TA145175
	Moated Site	TA 144179
	Moated Site	TA 143182

	DMV Of Lobingham	TA 143183
Redbourne	Socketed Axe	SK 975997
	Socketed Axe	SK 97459999
	Socketed Spearhead	SK 99828904
	Roman Pottery	SK 970988
	Moated Site	SK 977999
	Motte & Bailey	SK 974999
	Moated Site	TF 002997
	Medieval Priory	SE 998002
	Ring Ditch	SK 961988
	Rectangular Enclosure	SK 957992
	Complex Settlement	SK 978982

	Enclosure	SK 992989
	Enclosure	SK 968981
	Flanged Axe	TF 002997
	Palstave Axe	TF 002997
Roxby Cum Risby	Roman Site	SE 91581563
	Roman Kiln Wasters	SE 91151595
	Roman Pottery	SE 912158
	Roman Kilns	SE 90771402
	Roman Villa	SE 92031696
	Roman Pottery	SE 92021697
	Roman Coins	SE 92101694
		SE 92141688

	DMV Of Sawliffe	SE 911144
	Medieval Pottery	SE 908143
	Dagger Chape	SE 90981402
	DMV Of Risby	SE 921147
	DMV Of Low Risby	SE 930149
	Groat Of Edward IV	SE 931165
	Enclosures	SE 915160
	Complex Site	SE 927166
Saxby All Saints	Moated Site	SE 98951685
Scawby	Multi Period Finds	SE 973054
		SE 974055
	Roman Site	SE 975060

Roman Site	SE 949049
Roman Building	SE 951057
Roman Stone Coffin	SE 956053
Roman Pottery	SE 951043
Roman Villa	SE 96900465
Roman Pottery	SE 979045
Trumpet Brooch	SE 96960492
Spectacle Buckle	SE 97690530
Rectilinear Enclosure	SE 974057
Roman Buildings	SE 964041
Enclosure	SE 974057

South Ferriby	**Colossal Amount Of Finds**	
	Recovered From Cliff Areas	
	Along Anchome Valley	
	Centred On The Numbers	**SE 993217**
		SE 997206
		TA 001224
		SE 99302173
		SE 988214

Thousands Of Brooches & Artefacts Found

Including Many Roman Coins & Gold Staters

From Above Sites

	Moated Site	**SE 985208**
	Rectangular Enclosure	**SE 982205**
South Killingholme	**Moated Site**	**TA 148165**

Thornton Curtis	**Barrow**	**TA 055173**
	DMV Of Burnham	**TA 059171**
	Thornton Abbey	**TA 117189**
	Roman Pottery	**TA 034162**
Ulceby	**High Status IA Finds Including**	**TA 121161**
	Silver/Gold Harness Decorations	
	With Many Other Items In Form Of	
	Llyn Cerrig Trumpet	**TA 123156**
West Halton	**Bronze Axes x 17**	**SE 91222057**
	Roman Pottery	**SE 882193**
	Medieval Pottery	**SE 904209**
	DMV Of Haythby	**SE 883193**
	Moated Site	**SE 898198**
	Enclosure	**SE 907216**

	Ring Ditch	SE 911217
	Ring Ditches	SE 902198
Whitton	Roman Pottery	SE 91122418
	Roman Coins	SE 90232419
		SE 899244
Winteringham	Barrow	SE 92452168
	Roman Settlement	SE 947214
	Coritani Stater	SE 945212
	Rectangular Enclosure	SE 926208
	Rectangular Enclosure	SE 942219
	Circular Enclosure	SE 923295
Winterton	Roman Coins	SE 91891857

SE 924183

Roman Kilns	SE 93201915
Roman Coins	SE 942194
Roman Villa	SE 911182
Roman Pottery	SE 913180
Large Enclosure	SE 922189
Enclosure	SE 922189
Complex Site	SE 916187
Rectangular Enclosure	SE 915195
Complex Site	SE 920195
Circular Enclosure	SE 923180
Ring Ditch	SE 920192

Wootton	Round Barrow	TA07631510
	Round Barrow	TA 09531525
	DMV Of Wootton	TA 090161
Worlaby	Roman Villa	TA 017143
	Medieval Spindle Whorl	TA 014136
	Medieval Pottery	TA 01821417
	Double Enclosure	TA 006145
	Enclosure	TA 022139
Wrawby	Haft Flanged Axe	TA 02381058
	Roman Building	TA 018078
	Medieval Pottery	TA 021087

Grimsby

Barrow	**TA 27790886**
Barrow	**TA 28160870**
Rectangular Enclosure	**TA 276076**
Gold Staters x 6	**TA 26680707**
Gold Staters x 4	**TA26480838**
Roman Coin	**TA 265099**
Roman Pottery	**TA 250085**
Roman Coin	**TA 26580902**
Roman Pottery	**TA 24270863**
Spindle Whorl	**TA 24590895**
DMV Of Weelsby	**TA 280074**

Roman Pottery	TA 263064
Wellow Abbey	TA 269087
St Leonards Priory	TA 265079
Grey Friars Friary	TA 264090
Austin Friary	TA 269094
St Magdelene Hospital	TA 264086
Moated Site	TA 29080829
Moated Site	TA 233097

Scunthorpe

Flat Axe	SE 892079
Roman Pottery	SE 888086
Lead Human Head	SE 90760838

Roman Coins	SE 905087
Socketed Axe	SE 905100
Medieval Pottery	SE 891096
Rectangular Enclosure	SE 880120
Socketed Axe	SE 887138
DMV Of Little Conesby	SE 896137
Moated Site	SE 88161444
DMV Of Great Conesby	SE 896137
Roman Brooches	SE 896143
Roman Coins	SE 898118
IA Settlement	SE 905138
Socketed Spearhead	SE 910110

ROMAN VILLA'S

Bedfordshire

Colworth	Roman Villa	SP 971603
Tottenhoe	Roman Villa	SP 98932080

Berkshire

Aldermaston	Roman Villa	SU 605681
Basildon	Roman Villa	SU 60797929
Marlston	Roman Villa	SU 529738
Cox Green	Roman Villa	SU 86877979
Yattendon	Roman Villa	SU 53237523
Kintbury	Roman Villa	SU 39416715
Upper Lambourn	Roman Villa	SU 301828

Pangbourne	Roman Villa	SU 61757378
Maidenhead	Roman Villa	SU 88068110
Hermitage	Roman Villa	SU 52347258

Buckinghamshire

Stantonbury	Roman Villa	SP 82714036
Foscott	Roman Villa	SP 72233530
Hambleden	Roman Villa	SP 78638483
High Wycombe	Roman Villa	SP 87409239
Latimer	Roman Villa	SP 899779852
Lavendon	Roman Villa	SP 90895409
Mursley	Roman Villa	SP 83263038
Saunderton	Roman Villa	SP 79710190

Stantonbury	Roman Villa	SP 841430
Thornton	Roman Villa	SP 75653672

Cambridgeshire

Barnack	Roman Villa	TF 08030663
Bartlow	Roman Villa	TL 58724499
Castor	Roman Villa	TL 12609725
Comberton	Roman Villa	TL 38455489
Croydon	Roman Villa	TL 324483
Fordham	Roman Villa	TL 635684
Godmanchester	Roman Villa	TL 257713
Great Wilbraham	Roman Villa	TL 55825763
Guilden Morden	Roman Villa	TL 27634054

Helpston	Roman Villa	TF 12370408
Huntingdon	Roman Villa	TL 23667138
Ickleton	Roman Villa	TL 496431
Walton	Roman Villa	TF 182020
Linton	Roman Villa	TL 57594515
Littlington	Roman Villa	TL 31264247
Orton Longueville	Roman Villa	TL 176956
Barnack	Roman Villa	TF 05670651
Reach	Roman Villa	TL 57266518
Great Staughton	Roman Villa	TL 13466304
Thornhaugh	Roman Villa	TF 07630046

Teversham	Roman Villa	TL 49965752
Water Newton	Roman Villa	TL 111973

Cheshire

Eaton	Roman Villa	SJ 571634

Cornwall

Illogan	Roman Villa	SW 63674235

Derbyshire

Carsington Water	Roman Villa	SK 24925166

Devon

Downes Crediton	Roman Villa	SX 85049920
Holcombe	Roman Villa	SY 31499281

Seaton	Roman Villa	SY 238909

Dorset

Corfe Castle	Roman Villa	SY 97898272
Dewlish	Roman Villa	SY 76789720
East Creech	Roman Villa	SY 93478277
Fifehead Neville	Roman Villa	ST 77281121
Frampton	Roman Villa	SY 61589528
Halstock	Roman Villa	ST 53380757
Witchampton	Roman Villa	ST 96320587
Hinton St Mary	Roman Villa	ST 78451602
Iwerne Minster	Roman Villa	ST 85691375

Sherborne	Roman Villa	ST 62451529
Gussage St Andrew	Roman Villa	ST 973143
Preston	Roman Villa	SY 70298270
Tarrant Hinton	Roman Villa	ST 92591194
Thornford	Roman Villa	ST 59451363
Charminster	Roman Villa	SY 66729492
Wynford Eagle	Roman Villa	SY 575952

Essex

Alresford	Roman Villa	TM 06091993
Ashdon	Roman Villa	TL 57784347
Brightlingsea	Roman Villa	TM 05881872
Chignal St James	Roman Villa	TL 66251086

Finchingfield	**Roman Villa**	**TL 668337**
		TL 69053256
Fryerning	**Roman Villa**	**TL 646018**
Gestingthorpe	**Roman Villa**	**TL 827386**
Great Tey	**Roman Villa**	**TL 88922546**
Little Hallingbury	**Roman Villa**	**TL 49163822**
Harlow	**Roman Villa**	**TL 48091255**
Little Dunmow	**Roman Villa**	**TL 664212**
Little Oakley	**Roman Villa**	**TM 223290**
Mucking	**Roman Villa**	**TQ 673804**
Abberton	**Roman Villa**	**TL 994203**
Pleshey	**Roman Villa**	**TL 65101435**

Rivenhall	Roman Villa	TL 82971784
Ridgewell	Roman Villa	TL 73304026
Stebbing	Roman Villa	TL 67692446
		TL 68852334
Wendens Ambo	Roman Villa	TL 508360
West Mercia	Roman Villa	TM 00961251

Gloucestershire

Lower Swell	Roman Villa	SP 18542624
Ampney St Peter	Roman Villa	SP 08050052
Barnsley	Roman Villa	SP 08120617
Barrington	Roman Villa	SP 20411381
Bibury	Roman Villa	SP 12220652

Boughspring	**Roman Villa**	**ST 55969738**
Brislington	**Roman Villa**	**ST 61647097**
Broadwell	**Roman Villa**	**SP 19922802**
Chedworth	**Roman Villa**	**SP 05271347**
Upton Cheyney	**Roman Villa**	**ST 695698**
Cirencester	**Roman Villa**	**SP 01630232**
Farmington	**Roman Villa**	**SP 13231582**
Wick	**Roman Villa**	**ST 70667192**
Colesbourne	**Roman Villa**	**SO 98411107**
Compton Abdale	**Roman Villa**	**SP 04821624**
Woodmancote	**Roman Villa**	**SO 99590944**
Eastleach	**Roman Villa**	**SP 18900634**

Ebrington	Roman Villa	SP 18923999
Frocester	Roman Villa	SO 78490272
Barrington	Roman Villa	SP 21711324
Lechlade	Roman Villa	SP 21200249
Great Rissington	Roman Villa	SP 18941634
Great Witcombe	Roman Villa	SO 89931424
Painswick	Roman Villa	SO 85761021
Rodmanton	Roman Villa	ST 94439843
Hucclecote	Roman Villa	SO 87691755
Marshfield	Roman Villa	ST 79857602
Kempsford	Roman Villa	SU 16809711

Kings Weston	Roman Villa	ST 53397755
Lechlade	Roman Villa	SP 21600087
Bournes Green	Roman Villa	S0 91320438
Chedworth	Roman Villa	SP 07011174
Naunton	Roman Villa	SP 131234
Ayburton	Roman Villa	SO 62500187
Cromhall	Roman Villa	ST 68588974
Shipton	Roman Villa	SP 05471825
Winchcombe	Roman Villa	SP 04502568
Frocester	Roman Villa	SO 77100327
North Nibley	Roman Villa	ST 74139702
Woolaston	Roman Villa	ST 597987

Tockington	Roman Villa	ST 62728565
Tresham	Roman Villa	ST 803901
Turkdean	Roman Villa	SP 099190
Winchcombe	Roman Villa	SP 02332604
Whittington	Roman Villa	SP 00802093
Aldsworth	Roman Villa	SP 143101
Whittington	Roman Villa	SP 01562051
Sandhurst	Roman Villa	SO 83862425
Withington	Roman Villa	SP 03111486
Woodchester	Roman Villa	SO 83960311
Wortley	Roman Villa	ST 76909184

Greater London

Beddington	Roman Villa	TQ 29766581
Orpington	Roman Villa	TQ 45426583
Keston	Roman Villa	TQ 41316327
St Mary Cray	Roman Villa	TQ 46796758
Wanstead	Roman Villa	TQ 41858716

Hampshire

Abbotts Ann	Roman Villa	SU 31434190
Appleshaw	Roman Villa	SU 30164764
Upper Wootton	Roman Villa	SU 58005594
Binstead	Roman Villa	SU 786413
Bramdean	Roman Villa	SU 62752813

Burghclere	Roman Villa	SU 48286015
Clanville	Roman Villa	SU 21454897
Crondall	Roman Villa	SU 79504712
Eastleigh	Roman Villa	SU 45231628
Fullerton	Roman Villa	SU 37494006
Fyfield	Roman Villa	SU 29525028
Bentley	Roman Villa	SU 77914582
Grateley	Roman Villa	SU 276410
Hambledon	Roman Villa	SU 64431429
Havant	Roman Villa	SU 69150726
Hurstbourne Priors	Roman Villa	SU 44574982
Itchen Abbas	Roman Villa	SU 52883430

Langstone	Roman Villa	SU 71730532
West Meon	Roman Villa	SU 63212451
Longstock	Roman Villa	SU 34193617
Meonstoke	Roman Villa	SU 61652105
Micheldever	Roman Villa	SU 53093820
Monk Sherborne	Roman Villa	SU 60665486
North Waltham	Roman Villa	SU 56994549
Odiham	Roman Villa	SU 73615263
Old Alresford	Roman Villa	SU 58193342
Rockbourne	Roman Villa	SU 12011702
Rowlands Castle	Roman Villa	SU 73420988

Sparsholt	Roman Villa	SU 41493012
Chilton Candover	Roman Villa	SU 58044108
Stroud	Roman Villa	SU 72512360
Tidbury Ring	Roman Villa	SU 46284292
Twyford	Roman Villa	SU 48342439
Upham	Roman Villa	SU 54422247
Wyck	Roman Villa	SU 75873938

Herefordshire

Bishopstone	Roman Villa	SO 41754337
Credenhill	Roman Villa	SO 44654263
Goodrich	Roman Villa	SO 56431768
Kenchester	Roman Villa	SO 43674181

Radlett	Roman Villa	TL 143011
Radwell	Roman Villa	TL 23443535
Weston	Roman Villa	TL 27273079

Hertfordshire

Boxmoor	Roman Villa	TL 03810568
Welwyn	Roman Villa	TL 23551601
Hemel Hempstead	Roman Villa	TL 05030867
Gorhambury	Roman Villa	TL 11750793
Kings Langley	Roman Villa	TL 078022
Moor Park	Roman Villa	TQ 08009348
Northchurch	Roman Villa	SP 97300923
Park Street	Roman Villa	TL 14690308

Wymondley	Roman Villa	TL 29722924

Isle Of Wight

Brading	Roman Villa	SZ 60008625
Carisbrooke	Roman Villa	SZ 48508809
Robin Hill	Roman Villa	SZ 53808787
Gurnard	Roman Villa	SZ 47149540
Newport	Roman Villa	SZ 50118855
Brighstone	Roman Villa	SZ 42368415

Kent

Minster	Roman Villa	TR 31366463
New Ash Green	Roman Villa	TQ 60846500
Teynham	Roman Villa	TQ 94806409

Blean	**Roman Villa**	**TR 12866062**
Upchurch	**Roman Villa**	**TQ 85386626**
Cobham	**Roman Villa**	**TQ 68326932**
Darenth	**Roman Villa**	**TQ 56337064**
Dartford	**Roman Villa**	**TQ 54647345**
Eccles	**Roman Villa**	**TQ 72106061**
Farningham	**Roman Villa**	**TQ 55496674**
Faversham	**Roman Villa**	**TR 02086172**
Folkstone	**Roman Villa**	**TR 24083699**
Hartlip	**Roman Villa**	**TQ 82876403**
Luddenham	**Roman Villa**	**TQ 976626**
Lullingstone	**Roman Villa**	**TQ 53016508**

Maidstone	Roman Villa	TQ 75725621
Rodmersham	Roman Villa	TQ 92525982
Otford	Roman Villa	TQ 53625922
Plaxtol	Roman Villa	TQ 61485313
Sandwich	Roman Villa	TR 31905730
Snodland	Roman Villa	TQ 70756201
Teston	Roman Villa	TQ 69885316
Thurnham	Roman Villa	TQ 79785715
Wilmington	Roman Villa	TQ 54177299
Wingham	Roman Villa	TR 24055724

Leicestershire

Bringhurst	Roman Villa	SP 844921

Drayton	Roman Villa	SP 817918
Claybrooke Magna	Roman Villa	SP 481885
Glooston	Roman Villa	SP 75279603
Barkby Thorpe	Roman Villa	SK 647076
Lockington	Roman Villa	SK 480295
Lowesby	Roman Villa	SK 736068
Leicester	Roman Villa	SK 57530407
Medbourne	Roman Villa	SP 79829299
Osbaston	Roman Villa	SK 425038
Rothley	Roman Villa	SK 56901229
Sapcote	Roman Villa	SP 49679312
Drayton	Roman Villa	SP 83059310

West Langton	**Roman Villa**	**SP 71489207**
Goadby Marwood	**Roman Villa**	**SK 782255**

Lincolnshire

Hemingby	**Roman Villa**	**TF 24157331**
Denton	**Roman Villa**	**SK 87593094**
Glentworth	**Roman Villa**	**SK 94378828**
Kirton In Lindsey	**Roman Villa**	**SK 939966**
Haceby	**Roman Villa**	**TF 01953692**
Horkstow	**Roman Villa**	**SE 98491914**
Kirmond Le Mire	**Roman Villa**	**TF 183930**
Kirton In Lindsey	**Roman Villa**	**SE 93940038**

Norton Disney	Roman Villa	SK 85896028
Roxby	Roman Villa	SE 92031697
Scampton	Roman Villa	SK 95527847
Stainby	Roman Villa	SK 921222
Sudbrooke	Roman Villa	TF 037765
Walesby	Roman Villa	TF 14739262
Winterton	Roman Villa	SE 90961799

Norfolk

Bolwick Hall	Roman Villa	TG 205245
Feltwell	Roman Villa	TL 700921
Gayton		
Thorpe	Roman Villa	TF 73541806

Grimston	Roman Villa	TF 716216
Snettisham	Roman Villa	TF 68953370
Tivetshall St Mary	Roman Villa	TM 164843
Weeting	Roman Villa	TL 77808784

Northamptonshire

Apethorpe	Roman Villa	TL 02639493
Ashley	Roman Villa	SP 79409163
Daventry	Roman Villa	SP 58906321
Brixworth	Roman Villa	SP 74657187
Byfield	Roman Villa	SP 506545
Chipping Warden	Roman Villa	SP 51094822

Cosgrove	Roman Villa	SP 79474212
Cotterstock	Roman Villa	TL 03209101
Deanshanger	Roman Villa	SP 770396
Fotheringhay	Roman Villa	TL 07899446
Weldon	Roman Villa	SP 92948999
Harpole	Roman Villa	SP 68936209
Stanwick	Roman Villa	SP 97147179
Nether Heyford	Roman Villa	SP 66675865
Barnwell	Roman Villa	TL 07438368
Piddington	Roman Villa	SP 79785414
Quinton	Roman Villa	SP 775535
Ringstead	Roman Villa	SP 976748
Thenford	Roman Villa	SP 52524158

Stoke Bruerne	Roman Villa	SP 75465003
Whittlebury	Roman Villa	SP 73224457
Woollaston	Roman Villa	SP 90096488
Hunsbury Hill	Roman Villa	SP 737582
Yarwell	Roman Villa	TL 06189914

Nottinghamshire

Car Colston	Roman Villa	SK 71934248
Cromwell	Roman Villa	SK 802625
Barton In Fabis	Roman Villa	SK 52683166
Mansfield Woodhouse	Roman Villa	SK 52516455
Oldcotes	Roman Villa	SK 59098853

Southwell	Roman Villa	SK 70285378
Thurgarton	Roman Villa	SK 67344945

Oxfordshire

Asthall	Roman Villa	SP 30261120
Abingdon	Roman Villa	SU 510977
Ramsden	Roman Villa	SP 33931525
Stonesfield	Roman Villa	SP 40971943
Little Milton	Roman Villa	SP 62390030
Ditchley	Roman Villa	SP 39932008
Sutton Courtenay	Roman Villa	SU 49429389
Elsfield	Roman Villa	SP 54900895
Fawler	Roman Villa	SP 37171689

Frilford	**Roman Villa**	**SU 42289726**
Garford	**Roman Villa**	**SU 43709542**
Goring On Thames	**Roman Villa**	**SU 60007990**
Great Tew	**Roman Villa**	**SP 40502748**
Hanwell	**Roman Villa**	**SP 42864373**
Harpsden	**Roman Villa**	**SU 75658047**
Islip	**Roman Villa**	**SP 53251342**
North Leigh	**Roman Villa**	**SP 39701541**
Fawler	**Roman Villa**	**SP 37931667**
Stanford In The Vale	**Roman Villa**	**SU 32499510**
Stonesfield	**Roman Villa**	**SP 40031706**
West Challow	**Roman Villa**	**SU 37578789**

Wheatley	Roman Villa	SP 60580441
Wigginton	Roman Villa	SP 39363356
Widford	Roman Villa	SP 27791185
Woolstone	Roman Villa	SU 29048777

Rutland

Empingham	Roman Villa	SK 94280765
Great Casterton	Roman Villa	TF 00640955
Thistleton	Roman Villa	SK 90951717
Tixover	Roman Villa	SK 98150188

Shropshire

Acton Scott	Roman Villa	SO 45808977
Ashford Carbonell	Roman Villa	SO 53136932

Cruckton	**Roman Villa**	**SJ 43211017**
Shorthill	**Roman Villa**	**SJ 41760848**
Bayston Hill	**Roman Villa**	**SJ 45700963**
Harley	**Roman Villa**	**SJ 60650091**

Somerset

Banwell	**Roman Villa**	**ST 39825927**
Wraxall	**Roman Villa**	**ST 47877158**
Laverton	**Roman Villa**	**ST 765541**
Burnett	**Roman Villa**	**ST 66506454**
Bratton Seymour	**Roman Villa**	**ST 66702990**
Chew Magna	**Roman Villa**	**ST 588610**
Chew Valley Lake	**Roman Villa**	**ST 56885934**

East Coker	**Roman Villa**	**ST 54601377**
Combe Down	**Roman Villa**	**ST 76146219**
Compton		
Dundon	**Roman Villa**	**ST 49163104**
Dinnington	**Roman Villa**	**ST 404135**
Ham Hill	**Roman Villa**	**ST 48831649**
High Ham	**Roman Villa**	**ST 42182952**
Hurcott	**Roman Villa**	**ST 51132972**
Illchester	**Roman Villa**	**ST 51222213**
Farleigh		
Hungerford	**Roman Villa**	**ST 79735830**
Keynsham	**Roman Villa**	**ST 64516925**
Lopen	**Roman Villa**	**ST 427139**

Low Ham	Roman Villa	ST 43552884
Lufton	Roman Villa	ST 51511784
Leigh On Mendip	Roman Villa	ST 703475
Newton St Loe	Roman Villa	ST 71206553
Paulton	Roman Villa	ST 67125674
Pitney	Roman Villa	ST 450530O6
Priddy	Roman Villa	ST 53095146
Shapwick	Roman Villa	ST 42473948
Keynsham	Roman Villa	ST 65636894
Somerton	Roman Villa	ST 49712904
Wadeford	Roman Villa	ST 30881049
Wellow	Roman Villa	ST 72805799

Yatton	Roman Villa	ST 40526522
Yeovil	Roman Villa	ST 54881570
West Coker	Roman Villa	ST 528138
Whatley	Roman Villa	ST 74424699
Whitestaunton	Roman Villa	ST 28021058
Wincanton	Roman Villa	ST 70212819

Staffordshire

Acton Trussell	Roman Villa	SJ 937175
Hales	Roman Villa	SJ 72223371
Shenstone	Roman Villa	SK 11030544
Brewood	Roman Villa	SJ 89451023

Suffolk

Castle Hill	Roman Villa	TM 14744660
Exning	Roman Villa	TL 61216759
Farnham	Roman Villa	TM 37125836
Icklingham	Roman Villa	TL 78067204
Lidgate	Roman Villa	TL 73195715
Pakenham	Roman Villa	TL 90126950
Stanton	Roman Villa	TL 955742
Stonham Aspal	Roman Villa	TM 13095944

Surrey

Abinger	Roman Villa	TQ 10644746
Ashtead	Roman Villa	TQ 17756017

Banstead	**Roman Villa**	**TQ 22395567**
Fancombe	**Roman Villa**	**SU 970460**
Chiddingfold	**Roman Villa**	**SU 97843610**
Compton	**Roman Villa**	**SU 95734798**
Ewhurst	**Roman Villa**	**TQ 08034152**
Titsey Place	**Roman Villa**	**TQ 40485457**
Walton Heath	**Roman Villa**	**TQ 23165365**
Worplesdon	**Roman Villa**	**SU 96895107**

Sussex

Barcombe	**Roman Villa**	**TQ 417142**
Eastbourne	**Roman Villa**	**TV 618990**
Hartfield	**Roman Villa**	**TQ 44373195**

Plumpton	Roman Villa	TQ 360147
Beddingham	Roman Villa	TQ 45870734
Preston Park	Roman Villa	TQ 30910572
Angmering	Roman Villa	TQ 053104
Arundel	Roman Villa	TQ 01540692
Elsted	Roman Villa	SU 81801533
Bignor	Roman Villa	SU 98841469
Pulborough	Roman Villa	TQ 06882009
Chilgrove	Roman Villa	SU 84121362
Fishbourne	[Roman Palace]	SU 839404
H Pierpoint	Roman Villa	TQ 28091505
Littlehampton	Roman Villa	TQ 03960266

Worthing	Roman Villa	TQ 105038
Up Marden	Roman Villa	SU 797124
Sidlesham	Roman Villa	SZ 85479702
Southwick	Roman Villa	TQ 24460565
Walberton	Roman Villa	SU 978056
West Marden	Roman Villa	SU 77341264
Wiggonholt	Roman Villa	TQ 06471756

Warwickshire

Radford Semele	Roman Villa	SP 34256245
Long Itchington	Roman Villa	SP 39646685

Wiltshire

Allington	Roman Villa	SU 20693833

Atworth	Roman Villa	ST 85556640
Bedwyn	Roman Villa	SU 28356295
Box	Roman Villa	ST 82326854
Bradford On Avon	Roman Villa	ST 81756135
Brixton Deverill	Roman Villa	ST 86183884
Bromham	Roman Villa	ST 97086620
Marlborough	Roman Villa	SU 19296785
Chiseldon	Roman Villa	SU 19428095
Colerne	Roman Villa	ST 811718
Downton	Roman Villa	SU 18142106
E Grimstead	Roman Villa	SU 23372748
Hannington	Roman Villa	SU 18099585

Devizes	Roman Villa	SU 028629
Littlecote Park	Roman Villa	SU 30017055
Manningford	Roman Villa	SU 14025805
Netheravon	Roman Villa	SU 14764815
Sandy Lane	Roman Villa	ST 96936832
Sutton Veny	Roman Villa	ST 900433
Froxfield	Roman Villa	SU 27996960
Sherston	Roman Villa	ST 85558670
Stanton Fitzwarren	Roman Villa	SU 17329020
Stanton St Quintin	Roman Villa	ST 89607962
Bishopstone	Roman Villa	SU 25928158

Tockenham	Roman Villa	SU 03887971
Ford	Roman Villa	ST 83687609
West Dean	Roman Villa	SU 25792710

Worcestershire

Droitwich Spa	Roman Villa	SO 897638

Yorkshire

Brantingham	Roman Villa	SE 93152880
Grindale	Roman Villa	TA 13457122
Harpham	Roman Villa	TA 08996360
Rudston	Roman Villa	TA 08946671
S Newbald	Roman Villa	SE 90453610
Beadlam	Roman Villa	SE 63428412

N Stainley	Roman Villa	SE 29137559
Dalton On Tees	Roman Villa	NZ 30080822
Hovingham	Roman Villa	SE 66237569
Gargrave	Roman Villa	SD 93955351
Langton	Roman Villa	SE 81646750
Middleham	Roman Villa	SE 13468722
Manfield	Roman Villa	NZ 221152
Ingleby Barwick	Roman Villa	NZ 437150
Kirkby Wharfe	Roman Villa	SE 50564094
Well	Roman Villa	SE 26498182
Wharram Le Street	Roman Villa	SE 847656

		SE 868662
Wadworth	Roman Villa	SK 60979604
Collingham	Roman Villa	SE 40274453

Wales

Abermagwr	Roman Villa	SN 66887418
Caerwent	Roman Villa	ST 47549114
Llanddowror	Roman Villa	SN 25371213
Newton	Roman Villa	SS 84017802
Ely	Roman Villa	ST 14727615
Caerwent	Roman Villa	ST 44609101
Wolfscastle	Roman Villa	SM 94962647
Langstone	Roman Villa	ST 38398954

Llandough	Roman Villa	ST 168733
Llantwit Major	Roman Villa	SS 95886998
Llangadog	Roman Villa	SN 70492545
Amroth	Roman Villa	SN 17500785
Dyffryn	Roman Villa	ST 08117133

DESERTED MEDIEVAL VILLAGES

Berkshire

Littleworth	DMV	SU 320979
Shrivenham	DMV	SU 246892
Lockinge	DMV	SU 431868
Lambourn	DMV	SU 335782

Hungerford	DMV	SU 340698
Clapcot	DMV	SU 605916
Bray	DMV	SU 880740
Compton	DMV	SU 525796
Longworth	DMV	SU 400994
Eaton H	DMV	SU 260982
Fulscot	DMV	SU 545888
Henwick	DMV	SU 498686
Hill End	DMV	SU 466065
Hodcot	DMV	SU 477818
Kintbury	DMV	SU 401645
Langley	DMV	SU 498766

Maidencourt	DMV	SU 373760
Marlston	DMV	SU 529719
Newton	DMV	SU 529719
Ashbury	DMV	SU 271862
Purley P	DMV	SU 654769
Wytham	DMV	SP 486075
Brimpton	DMV	SU 569648
Burghfield	DMV	SU 653693
E Shefford	DMV	SU 391747
Southcote	DMV	SU 375910
Shottesbrook	DMV	SU 842771
Cumnor	DMV	SU 444075

Radley	DMV	SU 518973
Appleton	DMV	SP 446010
Whatcombe	DMV	SU 393789
Cumnor	DMV	SP 442053
Wooley	DMV	SU 410800
Hampstead N	DMV	SU 543760

Buckinghamshire

Frief	DMV	SU 807907
Oakley	DMV	SP 665113

Dorset

Chaldon Herring	DMV	SY 7706983265
Okeford Fitzpaine	DMV	ST 799118

Puddletown	DMV	SY 7664894770
Whitcombe	DMV	SY 7169688305
Winterborne F	DMV	SY 6981788240

Hertfordshire

Alswick	DMV	TL 476295
Beauchamps	DMV	TL 382314
Aldwick	DMV	SP 892175
Aspenden	DMV	TL 347288
Ayot		
St Lawrence	DMV	TL 194169
Berkenden	DMV	TL 335276
Boxbury	DMV	TL 274266
Betlow	DMV	SP 897172

Bozen Green	**DMV**	**TL 412272**
Brickenden	**DMV**	**TL 330105**
Burston	**DMV**	**TL 135037**
Broadfield	**DMV**	**TL 325310**
Broadmead	**DMV**	**SP 892175**
Caldecote	**DMV**	**TL 237385**
Chaldean	**DMV**	**TL 423205**
Chesfield	**DMV**	**TL 247278**
Childwick	**DMV**	**TL 141107**
Cockenach	**DMV**	**TL 396302**
Cockhamstead	**DMV**	**TL 419253**
Corney Bury	**DMV**	**TL 358307**

Digswell	DMV	TL 236149
Flaunden	DMV	TL 009988
Flexmere	DMV	TL 168224
Gilston	DMV	TL 440135
Gt Munden	DMV	TL 355243
Gubblecote	DMV	SP 905192
Hanstead	DMV	TL 143017
Hixham	DMV	TL 454268
Hodenhoe	DMV	TL 346334
Layston	DMV	TL 370300
Kitts End	DMV	TL 245984
Leverage	DMV	TL 435165

Libury	DMV	TL 345235
Mardley	DMV	TL 259185
Maydencroft	DMV	TL 182274
Minsden	DMV	TL 198246
Miswell	DMV	SP 912120
Moor Green	DMV	SP 321266
Napsbury	DMV	TL 165043
Nettleden	DMV	TL 015104
Newsells	DMV	TL 386372
North Mymms	DMV	TL 222045
Pendley	DMV	SP 944117
Plashes	DMV	TL 382203

Queenhoo	DMV	TL 278162
Quickswood	DMV	TL 278328
Stagenhoe	DMV	TL 186227
Stanstead A	DMV	TL 399110
Stevenage	DMV	TL 240262
Stocks	DMV	SP 962133
Stonebury	DMV	TL 384282
Temple Dinsley	DMV	TL 182248
Thorley	DMV	TL 476188
Throcking	DMV	TL 337303
Thundridge	DMV	TL 368175
Tiscott	DMV	SP 883178

Titburst	**DMV**	**TL 180995**
Wakerley	**DMV**	**TL 342269**
Wandon	**DMV**	**TL 132225**
Wellbury	**DMV**	**TL 142298**
Wickham	**DMV**	**TL 475230**
Windridge	**DMV**	**TL 125057**
Wollenwick	**DMV**	**TL 222253**

Gloucestershire

Blockley	**DMV**	**SP 1994436822**
Hartford	**DMV**	**SP 130225**
Naunton	**DMV**	**SP 130052248**

Kent

Buttdarts	DMV	TR 071296
Dode	DMV	TQ 669638
Eastbridge	DMV	TR 078319
Fairfield	DMV	TQ 977270
Falconhurst	DMV	TR 076344
Hampton On Sea	DMV	TR 156679
Hope All Saints	DMV	TR 049258
Midley	DMV	TR 016237
Orgarswick	DMV	TR 090309
Paddlesworth	DMV	TQ 624681
Shorne	DMV	TR 049258

Shuart	DMV	TR 2688067886
Snave	DMV	TR 015299

Leicestershire

Aldeby	DMV	SK 552987
Allhallows	DMV	SK 785361
Alton	DMV	SK 390148
Ambion	DMV	SK 400003
Andreskirk	DMV	SK 392222
Atterton	DMV	SP 353983
Baggrave	DMV	SK 697088
Beacon Hill	DMV	SK 513146
Beckingthorpe	DMV	SK 808394

Berehill	DMV	SK 587046
Bescaby	DMV	SK 823623
Bigging	DMV	SK 580062
Bishops Fee	DMV	SK 505051
Bradgate	DMV	SK 535103
Bradley	DMV	SP 823954
Brascote	DMV	SK 443025
Brentingby	DMV	SK 784198
Braunstone	DMV	SK560040
Brooksby	DMV	SK 670160
Bulwarks	DMV	SK 405233
Burrough Hill	DMV	SK 770120

Burrowchurch	**DMV**	**SK 835185**
Canby	**DMV**	**SK 606170**
Colby	**DMV**	**SK 617090**
Cold Newton	**DMV**	**SK 716065**
Gilmorton	**DMV**	**SP 553887**
Dishley	**DMV**	**SK 513212**
Doveland	**DMV**	**SK 560043**
Ullesthorpe	**DMV**	**SP 495870**
Elmesthorpe	**DMV**	**SP 460965**
Eye Kettleby	**DMV**	**SK 734167**
Foston	**DMV**	**SP 604950**
Groby	**DMV**	**SK 575054**

Frisby	DMV	SK 704020
Frogmire	DMV	SK 581052
Gerendon	DMV	SK 502199
Somerby	DMV	SK 770100
Gilroes	DMV	SK 560065
Goadby Marwood	DMV	SK 780270
Twycross	DMV	SK 353064
Great Stretton	DMV	SK 657005
Barkby Thorpe	DMV	SK 645075
Hardwick	DMV	SP 720970
Stockerston	DMV	SP 845957
Theddingworth	DMV	SP 669851

Wigston Magna	**DMV**	**SP 625985**
Ingarsby	**DMV**	**SK 684055**
Tugby	**DMV**	**SP 765995**
Ashby	**DMV**	**SK 354166**
Knaptoft	**DMV**	**SP 626895**
Stonton Wyville	**DMV**	**SP 744943**
Pickwell	**DMV**	**SK 792136**
Higham	**DMV**	**SP 365958**
Lowesby	**DMV**	**SK 725078**
Lubbesthorpe	**DMV**	**SK 541011**
Witherley	**DMV**	**SP 330968**
Medbourne	**DMV**	**SP 796929**

Stockerston	DMV	SP 845957
Misterton	DMV	SP 556840
Naneby	DMV	SK 435025
Ashby Folville	DMV	SK 706120
Owston	DMV	SK 765090
New Parks	DMV	SK 560058
Normandy	DMV	SP 489995
N Marefield	DMV	SK 752088
Noseley	DMV	SP 733987
Slawston	DMV	SP 771995
Hungarton	DMV	SK 702065
Scalford	DMV	SK 776235

St Clement	DMV	SK 581048
St Leonard	DMV	SK 580055
M Harborough	DMV	SP 741875
St Michael	DMV	SK 584049
St Peter	DMV	SK 585047
Withcote	DMV	SK 786052
Skelthorpe	DMV	SK 545185
S Marefield	DMV	SK 746079
Stapleford	DMV	SK 813183
Staunton Harold	DMV	SK 379209
Beaumont Leys	DMV	SK 583078
Stormsworth	DMV	SP 583806

Sysonby	DMV	SK 739190
Catthorpe	DMV	SP 552795
Toston	DMV	SK 800370
Shawell	DMV	SK 542782
Cotesbach	DMV	SK 519822
Claybrook M	DMV	SK 474888
Welby	DMV	SK 725210
Sibson	DMV	SK 570300
Westcotes	DMV	SK 570300
Westerby	DMV	SP 675925
Orton	DMV	SK 303027
Westrill	DMV	SP 580800

Whatborough	DMV	SK 767060
Whenham	DMV	SK 725238
Whittington	DMV	SP 486083
Willesley	DMV	SK 340146
Willows	DMV	SK 660180
Wistow	DMV	SP 644958
Withcote	DMV	SK 797059
Woodcote	DMV	SK 354187
Wyfordby	DMV	SK 792189

Lincolnshire

Aunby	DMV	TF 022146
Banthorpe	DMV	TF 062110

Casewick	DMV	TF 077090
Casthorpe	DMV	SK 861357
Beckfield	DMV	TF 190927
Birthorpe	DMV	TF 105344
Brauncewell	DMV	TF 046524
Bruer	DMV	TF 008537
Bardney	DMV	TF 134718
Crofton	DMV	TF 055402
Dembleby	DMV	TF 038378
Dunsby	DMV	TF 039514
Edenham	DMV	TF 055245
Gainsthorpe	DMV	SK 955012

Ganthorpe	DMV	SK 924291
Dowsby	DMV	TF 101297
Hanby	DMV	TF 027316
Lenton	DMV	TF 030310
Newbo	DMV	SK 867382
N Cadeby	DMV	TF 271960
N Rauceby	DMV	TF 021463
S Rochford	DMV	SK 916284
Orford	DMV	TF 198946
Osgodby	DMV	TF 020280
Ouesby	DMV	TF 105343
Ringsthorpe	DMV	SK 927414

Roxton	**DMV**	**TF 16681275**
Sempringham	**DMV**	**TF 105328**
Scott Willoughby	**DMV**	**TF 052376**
Silk Willoughby	**DMV**	**TF 047031**
Skinnand	**DMV**	**SK 941575**
Southorpe	**DMV**	**TF 043248**
Swayfield	**DMV**	**SK 986227**
Waterton	**DMV**	**SE 857181**
W Laughton	**DMV**	**TF 074311**
Wyham	**DMV**	**TF 277951**
W Wykeham	**DMV**	**TF 217885**
E Wykeham	**DMV**	**TF 226882**

Wykeham	DMV	TF 120972

Norfolk

Alethorpe	DMV	TF 948313
Alvington	DMV	TG 147218
Anmer	DMV	TF 737294
Appleton	DMV	TF 705274
Apton	DMV	TM 313993
Arminghall	DMV	TG 253048
Ashby	DMV	TG 419158
Ashwicken	DMV	TF 698190
Babingley	DMV	TF 670263
Barmer	DMV	TF 813336

Barton Bendish	DMV	TF 718062
Bawsey	DMV	TF 663207
Bayfield	DMV	TG 050405
Beachamwell	DMV	TF 752054
Beeston St Andrew	DMV	TG 251146
Bickerston	DMV	TG 086087
Bixley	DMV	TG 257040
Boyland	DMV	TM 222943
Bowthorpe	DMV	TG 177091
Breydeston	DMV	TG 341088
Brettenham	DMV	TL 939844
Broomsthorpe	DMV	TF 852289

Browston	DMV	TG 499017
Brumstead	DMV	TG 370265
Buckenham	DMV	TL 838947
Burgh Castle	DMV	TG 476043
Burgh On Aylsham	DMV	TG 218251
Burgh Parva	DMV	TG 044335
Bylaugh	DMV	TG 036184
Caistor St Edmund	DMV	TG 231035
Caldecote	DMV	TF 745034
Cantley	DMV	TG 181046
Carleton Forehoe	DMV	TG 094058

Choseley	DMV	TF 755408
Cley St Peter	DMV	TF 804044
Colveston	DMV	TL 794955
Cranwich	DMV	TL 783949
Didlington	DMV	TL 779970
Dunham	DMV	TF 986248
Dunton	DMV	TF 881300
Earlham	DMV	TG 193082
Eaton	DMV	TF 699362
Eccles	DMV	TG 414288
Egmere	DMV	TF 897374
Felbrigg	DMV	TG 197390

Foston	DMV	TF 652094
Frenze	DMV	TM 135804
Gasthorpe	DMV	TL 983813
Gayton	DMV	TF 719195
Glorestorp	DMV	TF 695182
Godwick	DMV	TF 903220
Gt Barwick	DMV	TF 807351
Gt Palgrave	DMV	TF 834120
Gt Snarehill	DMV	TL 893835
Grenstein	DMV	TF 907198
Gunton	DMV	TG 230340
Hales	DMV	TM 380960

Harlingthorpe	**DMV**	**TL 946842**
Hargham	**DMV**	**TM 020914**
Heckingham	**DMV**	**TM 385988**
Herringby	**DMV**	**TG 446103**
Hethel	**DMV**	**TG 172004**
Hockwold	**DMV**	**TL 723877**
Holkham	**DMV**	**TF 882430**
Holme	**DMV**	**TF 909069**
Holt	**DMV**	**TF 675184**
Holverston	**DMV**	**TG 307031**
Houghton	**DMV**	**TF 794285**
Houghton On The Hill	**DMV**	**TF 868053**

Illington	DMV	TL 946901
Ingloss	DMV	TM 345967
Irmingland	DMV	TG 123294
Kempstone	DMV	TF 886160
Kenningham	DMV	TM 206999
Kilverstone	DMV	TL 894841
Langford	DMV	TL 839965
Letton	DMV	TF 974097
Leziate	DMV	TF 695199
Little Appleton	DMV	TF 710210
Little Bittering	DMV	TF 935175
Little Brecles	DMV	TL 968937

Little Hockham	DMV	TL 949910
Little Palgrave	DMV	TF 832135
Little Snarehill	DMV	TL 889805
Little Wacton	DMV	TM 180902
L Witchingham	DMV	TG 117204
L Wreningham	DMV	TM 155980
Lynford	DMV	TL 820941
Maidenhouse	DMV	TF 597199
Maideston	DMV	TG 248216
Mannington	DMV	TG 144320
Markshill	DMV	TG 226047
Matlask	DMV	TG 152349

Middle Harling	DMV	TL 980851
Middleton	DMV	TF 803359
Mintlyn	DMV	TF 657192
Morley St Peter	DMV	TF 065984
N Barsham	DMV	TF 917349
North Lynn	DMV	TF 613211
Oby	DMV	TG 415144
O Fulmodeston	DMV	TF 996302
Panworth	DMV	TF 896048
Pattesley	DMV	TF 899241
Pensthorpe	DMV	TF 947290
Pockthorpe	DMV	TG 128063

Pudding Norton	**DMV**	**TF 924277**
Quarles	**DMV**	**TF 884385**
Rackheath	**DMV**	**TG 278152**
Rainthorpe	**DMV**	**TM 202972**
Ringstead Parva	**DMV**	**TF 684399**
Ristuna	**DMV**	**TF 622017**
Roudham	**DMV**	**TL 956872**
Rougham	**DMV**	**TF 825207**
Roxham	**DMV**	**TL 638997**
Santon	**DMV**	**TL 828873**
Thorpe Shotford	**DMV**	**TM 230966**
Shotesham	**DMV**	**TM 251821**

St Mary	DMV	TM 238988
Shouldham	DMV	TF 680089
Snore	DMV	TL 624993
Southgate	DMV	TG 137245
Southmere	DMV	TF 748385
Southwood	DMV	TG 393053
Sparham	DMV	TF 874111
Stanford	DMV	TL855946
Stanninghall	DMV	TG 255175
Stinton	DMV	TG 118255
Sturston	DMV	TL 875950
Sutton	DMV	TF 895206

Swathing	DMV	TF 986058
Testerton	DMV	TF 934267
Thorpe Parva	DMV	TM 161794
Thorpland	DMV	TF 616083
Threxton	DMV	TF 885001
Thurton	DMV	TG 100214
Thuxton	DMV	TG 035075
Toimere	DMV	TF 655066
Tottington	DMV	TL 893955
Twanton	DMV	TM 175929
Wallington	DMV	TF 626076
Washingford	DMV	TM 334992

Waterden	DMV	TF 887364
Wendling	DMV	TF 929122
W Harling	DMV	TL 975852
W Lexham	DMV	TF 843171
West Tofts	DMV	TL 837928
Wilby	DMV	TM 032900
W Wretham	DMV	TL 900914
Windle	DMV	TM 427939
Winston	DMV	TM 401931
Wolterton	DMV	TG 164324
Wyveiling	DMV	TF 692205

Oxfordshire

Asthall	DMV	SP 30261120
Abingdon	DMV	SU 510977
Ramsden	DMV	SP 33931525
Stonesfield	DMV	SP 4097193
Little Milton	DMV	SP 62390030
Ditchley	DMV	SP 39932008
Sutton Courtney	DMV	SU 49429389
Elsfield	DMV	SP 54900895
Fawler	DMV	SP 37171689
Frilford	DMV	SU 42289726
Garford	DMV	SU 43709542

Gatehampton	DMV	SU 60007990
Great Tew	DMV	SP 40502748
Hanwell	DMV	SP 42864373
Harpsden	DMV	SU 75658047
Islip	DMV	SP 53251342
North Leigh	DMV	SP 39701541
Fawler	DMV	SP 37931667
Stanford In The Vale	DMV	SU 32499510
Stonesfield	DMV	SP 40031706
West Challow	DMV	SU 37578789
Wheatley	DMV	SP 60580441
Wigginton	DMV	SP 39363356

Widford	DMV	SP 27791185
Woolstone	DMV	SU 29048777

Nottinghamshire

Adbolton	DMV	SK 600384
Algarthorpe	DMV	SK 555425
Annesley	DMV	SK 504524
Babworth	DMV	SK 685809
Beesthorpe	DMV	SK 730605
Bilby	DMV	SK 639832
Bingham	DMV	SK 714397
Bolham	DMV	SK 704826
Broadbusk	DMV	SK 688480

Broxstowe	**DMV**	**SK 527427**
Carburton	**DMV**	**SK 611733**
Clowne	**DMV**	**SK 579737**
Clumber	**DMV**	**SK 627747**
Colston Basset	**DMV**	**SK 695338**
Over Colwick	**DMV**	**SK 602390**
Cratley	**DMV**	**SK 666640**
Dallington	**DMV**	**SK 778429**
Danethorpe	**DMV**	**SK 842577**
E Chilwell	**DMV**	**SK 540380**
East Stoke	**DMV**	**SK 748501**
Farworth	**DMV**	**SK 629894**

Flawford	**DMV**	**SK 593332**
Fleecethorpe	**DMV**	**SK 629836**
Gleadthorpe	**DMV**	**SK 592701**
Greasley	**DMV**	**SK 489471**
Grimston Hill	**DMB**	**SK 682658**
Haughton	**DMV**	**SK 692730**
Hempshill	**DMV**	**SK 525441**
Hermeston	**DMV**	**SK 589884**
Holbeck	**DMV**	**SK 658527**
Holme P	**DMV**	**SK 624393**
Horsepool	**DMV**	**SK 706478**
Keighton	**DMV**	**SK 542382**

Kilvington	DMV	SK 801429
Kinoulton	DMV	SK 662304
Knapthorpe	DMV	SK 740588
Langford	DMV	SK 822591
Little Gringley	DMV	SK 734811
Meering	DMV	SK 818655
Milnthorpe	DMV	SK 578723
Moorhouse	DMV	SK 753667
Morton In Babworth	DMV	SK 677801
Morton In Lenton	DMV	SK 547373
Nettleworth	DMV	SK 549658

Normanton	DMV	SK 650747
Osberton	DMV	SK 624800
Ossington	DMV	SK 760650
Oswaldbeck	DMV	SK 777855
Plumtree	DMV	SK 632923
Rayton	DMV	SK 615793
Rempstone	DMV	SK 575245
Rufford	DMV	SK 657641
Serlby	DMV	SK 633895
S Wheatley	DMV	SK 767856
Stanton On The Wolds	DMV	SK 631307
Sutton Passeys	DMV	SK 530390

Swanston	DMV	SK 810750
Thoresby	DMV	SK 648712
Thorney	DMV	SK 860726
Thorpe In The Glebe	DMV	SK 607258
Tiln	DMV	SK 703842
Wainscarre	DMV	SK 615877
Wansley	DMV	SK 461515
Warby	DMV	SK 633324
Welham	DMV	SK 727822
West Burton	DMV	SK 798855
Whimpton	DMV	SK 795740

Willoughby		
By Norwell	**DMV**	**SK 788632**
Willoughby		
By Walesby	**DMV**	**SK 689708**
Winkerfield	**DMV**	**SK 630606**
Wiverton	**DMV**	**SK 715365**
Woodcoates	**DMV**	**SK 655464**
	Rutland	
Empingham	**DMV**	**SK 94280765**
GT Casterton	**DMV**	**TF 00640955**
Thistleton	**DMV**	**SK 90951717**
Tixover	**DMV**	**SK 98150188**

Sussex

Apuldram	DMV	SU 838033
Balmer	DMV	TQ 360100
Balsdean	DMV	TQ 378040
Barpham	DMV	TQ 070093
Binderton	DMV	SU 847107
Burton	DMV	SU 968176
Charlton	DMV	SZ 880972
Cudlow	DMV	TQ 024005
E Itchenor	DMV	SZ 796996
Erringham	DMV	TQ 207078
Ford	DMV	TQ 003037

Hangleton	DMV	TQ 272078
Heene	DMV	TQ 138027
Kingston Buci	DMV	TQ 236053
Lordington	DMV	SU 781098
Lowfield Heath	DMV	TQ 249400
Manxey	DMV	TQ 651070
Monkton	DMV	SU 824150
Northeye	DMV	TQ 681070
Old Shoreham	DMV	TQ 21400575
Pangdean	DMV	TQ 294116
Parham	DMV	TQ 060140
Perching	DMV	TQ 242103

Poyningstown	DMV	TV 504986
Southerham	DMV	TQ 429093
S Heighton	DMV	TQ 451030
Stanmer	DMV	TQ 21400575
Streethill	DMV	TQ 357122
The Lydds	DMV	TQ 428034
Tidemills	DMV	TQ 460002

Shropshire

Acton Scott	DMV	SO 45808977
Ashford		
Carbonell	DMV	SO 53136932
Cruckton	DMV	SJ 43211017
Abdon	DMV	SO 576866

Acton Burnell	DMV	SJ 528021
Acton Piggott	DMV	SJ 542028
Acton Reynald	DMV	SJ 535230
Adlaston	DMV	SO 725935
Albright Hussey	DMV	SJ 501175
Allcott	DMV	SJ 511011
Allfield	DMV	SJ 503071
Amaston	DMV	SJ 378112
Annscroft	DMV	SJ 453077
Apley	DMV	SJ 654132
Arlescott	DMV	SJ 653007
Ashfield	DMV	SO 587893

Ashford		
Carbonell	**DMV**	**SO 525703**
Ashford Jones	**DMV**	**SO 528718**
Astley	**DMV**	**SO 781855**
Aston Botterell	**DMV**	**SO 632843**
Aston On Clun	**DMV**	**SO 396814**
Balsoms Heath	**DMV**	**SO 546883**
Bancroft	**DMV**	**SO 351794**
Bank	**DMV**	**SJ 465010**
Baucott	**DMV**	**SO 540873**
Baveney	**DMV**	**SO 689795**
Bayston Hill	**DMV**	**SJ 4950800**
Bearstone	**DMV**	**SJ 724397**

Belswardyne	DMV	SJ 6033033
Belton	DMV	SJ 528407
Benthall	DMV	SJ 394139
Berelawe	DMV	SJ 342107
Berley	DMV	SJ 317141
Berwick M	DMV	SJ 540105
Besford	DMV	SJ 551250
Beslow	DMV	SJ 580087
Betchcott	DMV	SO 437985
Betton Abbotts	DMV	SJ 515079
Betton Alkmere	DMV	SJ 505090
Betton In Hales	DMV	SJ 692370

Betton Strange	DMV	SJ 507093
Bettws y Crwyn	DMV	SO 178819
Billingsley	DMV	SO 705855
Binweston	DMV	SJ 301041
Bishton	DMV	SJ 804018
Bitterley	DMV	SO 571771
Blakemoor Flat	DMV	SJ 374008
Blakemoor Gate	DMV	SJ 374011
Blakeway	DMV	SO 595994
Bockleton	DMV	SO 578834
Bold	DMV	SO 640848
Boreton	DMV	SJ 513077

Bradley	**DMV**	**SO 616816**
Braggington	**DMV**	**SJ 336139**
Bratton	**DMV**	**SJ 637142**
Bridgwalton	**DMV**	**SO 687927**
Broadward	**DMV**	**SO 394768**
Brockleton	**DMV**	**SO 570830**
Brompton	**DMV**	**SJ 540079**
Bromwich	**DMV**	**SJ 319254**
Broncroft	**DMV**	**SO 546866**
Bronrotpol	**DMV**	**SJ 316126**
Brookhampton	**DMV**	**SO 567898**
Broom	**DMV**	**SJ 379317**

Broomcroft	DMV	SJ 568010
Broome	DMV	SO 525981
Broughton	DMV	SJ 497242
Burcot	DMV	SJ 622111
Burfield	DMV	SO 264803
Burford	DMV	SO 505682
Burley	DMV	SO 478814
Buttery	DMV	SJ 688171
Calcott Moss	DMV	SJ 448140
Calverhall	DMV	SJ 602372
Cantlop	DMV	SO 523058
Cantreyn	DMV	SO 713941

Castell Bryn

Amlwg	DMV	SO 167847
Catsley	DMV	SO 725796
Caurtune	DMV	SO 402856
Caus	DMV	SJ 338078
Charlcotte	DMV	SO 638861
Chelmick	DMV	SO 468914
Chipnall	DMV	SJ 727315
Chirbury B	DMV	SJ 282022
Chorley	DMV	SO 692834
Choulton	DMV	SO 378883
Church Stretton	DMV	SO 416893

Cleestanton	DMV	SO 574792
Clun	DMV	SO 302788
Clunbury	DMV	SO 351794
Coats	DMV	SO 526926
Coldgreene	DMV	SO 596820
Cold Weston	DMV	SO 552830
Colehurst	DMV	SJ 662314
Colemere	DMV	SJ 433327
Colstey Bank	DMV	SO 305841
Condover	DMV	SJ 495054
Corfham	DMV	SO 525850
Corfield	DMV	SO 570920

Coston	DMV	SO 386803
Cothercote	DMV	SJ 420016
Coton	DMV	SJ 531349
Cotton UponTern	DMV	SJ 631278
Cound	DMV	SJ 561053
Cressage	DMV	SJ 588044
Cresswell	DMV	SO 375767
Criddon	DMV	SO 666912
Crowsnest Dingle	DMV	SJ 375013
Darvill Grange	DMV	SJ 503137
Derrington	DMV	SO 607908
Detton	DMV	SO 667797

Deuxhill	DMV	SO 696872
Digbeth	DMV	SO 788937
Dingle Mill	DMV	SJ 297107
Ditherington	DMV	SJ 497138
Ditton Priors	DMV	SO 643900
Domas	DMV	SJ 594008
Donington	DMV	SJ 816050
Dothill	DMV	SJ 648130
Downton	DMV	SO 580800
Dudmaston	DMV	SO 745887
Dudston	DMV	SO 244975
Earls Ditton	DMV	SO 629756

Earnwood	DMV	SO 725803
Eastridge	DMV	SJ 390028
Eaton Mascott	DMV	SJ 538059
Edenhope	DMV	SO 158887
Edgeley	DMV	SJ 557402
Edstaston	DMV	SO 519319
Egerton	DMV	SO 605814
Emstrey	DMV	SJ 526105
Eudon Burnell	DMV	SO 699893
Eudon George	DMV	SO 689890
Eyton	DMV	SJ 377140
Faintree	DMV	SO 662890

Farley	DMV	SJ 388080
Farmcote	DMV	SO 785913
Fenemere	DMV	SJ 445230
F Alberbury	DMV	SJ 380135
Forton	DMV	SJ 430161
Fouswardine	DMV	SO 675856
Gippols	DMV	SO 582997
Golding	DMV	SJ 545035
Gonsal	DMV	SJ 480041
Gorham	DMV	SO 282753
Gravenhunger	DMV	SJ 743426
Great Oxenbold	DMV	SO 593519

Gretton	DMV	SO 517948
Halston	DMV	SJ 415078
Hampton Loade	DMV	SO 747864
Harcourt	DMV	SJ 570250
Harnage	DMV	SJ 569022
Hatton	DMV	SJ 766044
Haughton	DMV	SJ 553165
Hawcocks Mount	DMV	SJ 349077
Hayes	DMV	SJ 350154
Hayford	DMV	SJ 364103
Hayteley	DMV	SJ 513173
Heath	DMV	SO 557857

Heathway	DMV	SJ 282035
Henley	DMV	SO 543764
Hernegia	DMV	SJ 567004
Higford	DMV	SJ 754007
High Hatton	DMV	SJ 611248
Hisland	DMV	SJ 317272
Hobendrid	DMV	SO 309766
Hockleton	DMV	SJ 274301
Holdgate	DMV	SO 563894
Hollicot	DMV	SJ 439008
Holt Preen	DMV	SO 535966
Hopton	DMV	SJ 593267

Horton	DMV	SJ 439115
Hothales	DMV	SO 535995
Howle	DMV	SJ 691234
Hudwick	DMV	SO 630927
Humphreston	DMV	SJ 816050
Hundeslit	DMV	SJ 479945
Huntington	DMV	SO 537710
Idsall	DMV	SJ 744072
Ingardine	DMV	SO 628814
Isombridge	DMV	SJ 611138
Jackfield	DMV	SJ 685031
Kempton	DMV	SO 360830

Kenwick	**DMV**	**SJ 417305**
Kingsnordley	**DMV**	**SO 774877**
Kinlet	**DMV**	**SO 711911**
Kinson	**DMV**	**SO 577823**
Knowl	**DMV**	**SJ 731084**
Kynaston	**DMV**	**SJ 354202**
La Beche	**DMV**	**SJ 535051**
La Cresse	**DMV**	**SJ 470010**
Lackstone	**DMV**	**SO 573798**
Lacon	**DMV**	**SJ 539326**
Lake	**DMV**	**SJ 371069**
Langley	**DMV**	**SO 488803**

Larden	DMV	SO 568933
Lawley	DMV	SJ 668086
Lawton	DMV	SO 512838
Lea	DMV	SJ 41760848
Leaton	DMV	SJ 468185
Leebotwood	DMV	SO 470986
Leighton	DMV	SJ 613054
Leverdgrene	DMV	SO 595820
Little Berwick	DMV	SJ 473148
Little Hanwood	DMV	SJ 445077
Little Oxenbold	DMV	SO 587916
Little Parton	DMV	SJ 333110

Little Shrawardine	DMV	SJ 391150
Little Sutton	DMV	SO 513823
Little Tasker	DMV	SO 324961
Little Wollaston	DMV	SJ 376115
Longden	DMV	SJ 442063
Longner	DMV	SJ 528112
Longslow	DMV	SJ 655354
Lordshill	DMV	SJ 380019
Loton	DMV	SJ 356147
Lowe	DMV	SO 631805
Lower Bayston	DMV	SJ 492082

Lower Cleeton	DMV	SO 608792
Lower Cound	DMV	S0 558050
Lower Down	DMV	SO 336846
Lower Grounds	DMV	SJ 594158
Lower Ledwyche	DMV	SO 534736
Lower Millichope	DMV	SO 526878
Lower Newton	DMV	SJ 383084
Lydehole	DMV	SO 521820
Lydley	DMV	SO 483982
Maesbury	DMV	SJ 309257

Mainstone	DMV	SO 256863
Malehurst	DMV	SJ 383063
Marton	DMV	SJ 400090
Membrefield	DMV	SO 669939
Monk Hall	DMV	SO 613940
More	DMV	SO 564800
Moreton	DMV	SJ 567033
Moreton Corbet	DMV	SJ 558230
Neen Savage	DMV	SO 676786
Nethercott	DMV	SO 677785
Netley	DMV	SJ 467008

Newbold	DMV	SJ 557010
Newnham	DMV	SJ 411099
Newton	DMV	SJ 530050
Norncott	DMV	SO 565862
Norton	DMV	SJ 493071
Oldfield	DMV	SO 405830
Old Hardwick	DMV	SJ 367344
Old Shadwell	DMV	SO 262856
Padmore	DMV	SO 465794
Painston	DMV	SJ 447093
Pitchford	DMV	SJ 535052
Poulton	DMV	SJ 383055

Ramshurst	DMV	SJ 523000
Rea	DMV	SJ 360050
Ringmoreoak	DMV	SO 350986
Ruckley	DMV	SO 481804
Ruthall	DMV	SO 548824
Shipton	DMV	SO 562918
Sidnall	DMV	SO 643901
Siwaldston	DMV	SJ 580070
Smethcott	DMV	SO 452995
Sparchford	DMV	SO 496830
Stitt	DMV	SO 410985
Sutton On Tern	DMV	SJ 664310

The Yelds	DMV	SO 520820
Thorneton	DMV	SO 320734
Trilwardyne	DMV	SJ 734076
Whitley	DMV	SJ 45700963
Wicherley	DMV	SJ 588093
Wigley	DMV	SJ 370080
Witchcot	DMV	SO 533818
Woodmere	DMV	SJ 383152
Yarchester	DMV	SJ 60650091
Yeye	DMV	SO 490780

Warwickshire

Bedworth	DMV	SP 3502687506

Cestersover	**DMV**	**SP 504817**
Ettington	**DMV**	**SP 2737850220**
Fillongley	**DMV**	**SP 2583185804**
Stonelea	**DMV**	**SP 3272274582**
Stretton B	**DMV**	**SP 448818**
Wittybrook	**DMV**	**SP 4330884276**
Wolfhamcote	**DMV**	**SP 5289565465**
Wormleighton	**DMV**	**SP 4441954169**

Wiltshire

Calne	**DMV**	**SU 0030972892**
Grafton	**DMV**	**SU 2818760159**
Imber	**DMV**	**ST 965485**

Osmington	**DMV**	**SY 7486181642**
Woodsend	**DMV**	**SU 265756**

Printed in Great Britain
by Amazon

25149131R00126